"*Life on Delay* is not a disability memoir that focuses on trying to find a cure for stuttering, nor does it fall into the category of sentimental, inspirational stories of overcoming impossible odds. Instead, the book promotes a simple message: Obtaining true peace comes from accepting every part of yourself, including the things that bring you shame."

—*BookPage* (starred review)

"Powerful. . . . [Hendrickson's] interviews with researchers, therapists, fellow stutterers, and parents of children who stutter widen the narrative scope and compassionately uplift a stigmatized community. . . . This memoir casts a necessary light on a disability that too often goes unseen."

—*Publishers Weekly*

"A tremendous, and gorgeously written, memoir that will have you rooting for John—as well as catching glimpses of your own life's journey in his."   —Isaac Fitzgerald, *The Today Show*

"Deeply inspiring. . . . A congenial guide through the experiences of stutterers."   —*The National Book Review*

"Hendrickson's writing style has a vibrant immediacy to it that keeps you glued to the page."   —*Book and Film Globe*

"[Hendrickson writes] with profound intelligence and insight. . . . We've been waiting a long time for a book like this."   —*The Millions*

John Hendrickson

LIFE

ON

DELAY

John Hendrickson is a staff writer at *The Atlantic.*
He previously wrote and edited for *Rolling Stone,*
Esquire, and *The Denver Post.* His *Atlantic* feature
"What Joe Biden Can't Bring Himself to Say" was
named one of the best stories of 2019 by *Longform.*
He lives in New York City with his wife.

John Hendrickson is available for select speaking
engagements. To inquire about a possible appearance, please contact Penguin Random House Speakers Bureau at speakers@penguinrandomhouse.com
or visit prhspeakers.com.

LIFE
ON
DELAY

LIFE

ON

DELAY

Making Peace

with a Stutter

John Hendrickson

VINTAGE BOOKS

A DIVISION OF PENGUIN RANDOM HOUSE LLC

NEW YORK

FIRST VINTAGE BOOKS EDITION 2024

Grateful acknowledgment is made to the following for permission
to reprint previously published material: Hearst Magazine Media, Inc.:
Excerpts from "Letters Traveled by Sea," "A Life-Saver Vanished," and "A
Caffeine Fix Was Truly Needed" by John Hendrickson, originally published
in *Esquire* (2014). Reprinted by permission of Hearst Magazine Media,
Inc. · JJJJJerome Ellis: Excerpt from untitled reading by JJJJJerome Ellis,
originally performed as part of The Poetry Project's 46th Annual New
Year's Day Marathon at St. Mark's Church in 2020. · SC Publishing, d/b/a
Secretly Canadian Publishing: Lyric excerpt of "Farewell Transmission,"
lyrics written by Jason Molina, published by Autumn Bird Songs (ASCAP) /
Secretly Canadian Publishing (ASCAP). Reprinted by permission
of SC Publishing, d/b/a Secretly Canadian Publishing.

The Library of Congress has cataloged the Knopf edition as follows:
Names: Hendrickson, John, author.
Title: Life on delay: making peace with a stutter / John Hendrickson.
Description: First edition. | New York: Alfred A. Knopf, 2023.
Identifiers: LCCN 2021054996 (print) | LCCN 2021054997 (ebook)
Subjects: LCSH: Hendrickson, John (Atlantic senior editor)—Health.
| Stutterers—Biography. | Stuttering. | Stutterers—Maryland—Takoma
Park—Biography.
Classification: LCC RC424.H46 2023 (print) | LCC RC424 (ebook) |
DDC 616.85/540092 [B]—dc23/eng/20220121
LC record available at https://lccn.loc.gov/2021054996
LC ebook record available at https://lccn.loc.gov/2021054997

Vintage Books Trade Paperback ISBN: 978-0-593-31283-4
eBook ISBN: 978-0-593-31914-7

Book design by Betty Lew

vintagebooks.com

Printed in the United States of America
1st Printing

For Liz

The impediment to action advances action.
What stands in the way becomes the way.

—MARCUS AURELIUS

After tonight, if you don't want this to be
A secret out of the past
I will resurrect it, I'll have a good go at it

—SONGS: OHIA, "FAREWELL TRANSMISSION"

Contents

Author's Note

This book is based on dozens of interviews conducted over a two-year period. These discussions took place in person, over the phone, and across various audio/video platforms. All quotes have been edited for length and clarity. Many of these conversations concern memory. I have made a sincere effort to corroborate the events described in these stories through supplementary interviews, photographs, videos, emails, journal entries, newspaper clippings, and other forms of archival material, both on my own and with the help of a third-party fact-checker. While a large amount of the dialogue that appears in this text was recorded and transcribed, some of the quotes—namely pieces of dialogue from many years or decades ago—were reconstructed from my or other individuals' memory, which, by its very nature, is imperfect. I have done my best to write this book accurately and with empathy.

LIFE
ON
DELAY

1

Nothing in Your Hands

"You know, you don't have to do this," Jeff says. His voice has a fatherly tone. "You and I could get out of here. We could go get breakfast." He's kidding, but not really. If I say yes, Jeff will say okay, and we'll ride the elevator down to the lobby and not speak of it again. It will just be one of those days, another morning when I vanish rather than talk.

He leans against the makeup counter with his back to the mirror. My face is caked in concealer, but I can still see my acne scars, the dark circles under my eyes, my imperfect shave. I look scared, like a little boy getting a haircut who shrinks into the swivel chair as the clippers buzz toward his ears. Jeff is my boss; I can tell he's concerned. I want to take him up on his offer. I want to stand and leave and forget about all of this.

Eventually he says good-bye and good luck and pats my shoulder on his way out the door. I walk over to the little room where I'm supposed to wait. When I was young, my life was defined by little rooms. There was the speech therapist's office with the mysterious wall-length mirror. There was the windowless room in the basement of my elementary school. Everyone in class knew I went to the little room, but nobody wanted to bring it up. I never brought it up either, because maybe if I ignored the problem hard enough, it would disappear. That's what we were all hoping for—me, my mom, my dad, my brother. We've spent decades waiting for this strange thing to exit my body and drift away. For dozens of reasons, it has stuck around.

I've avoided almost anything resembling public speaking my entire life. But now I'm here, sweating through my shirt as the minutes tick by before they call me onto the set. My knee is bouncing uncontrollably. I'm staring at the floor, sipping a lukewarm black coffee that I struggled to order at Dunkin' Donuts earlier this morning. The cashier flashed me a familiar pity smile.

I stayed late at my office last night, sitting across the table from Helen, a public-relations person at my company. We entered a little room on the sixth floor and she turned on a fake newscaster voice to lead me in a mock interview. I couldn't get through one answer. She kept pushing me forward.

"Let's run through it again," she said.

"Okay, try again."

"Again?"

I couldn't start sentences. I'd break eye contact. I'd fiddle with a pen as a distraction to help me get to the next word. I wanted to leave, but she stayed, so I stayed. We began again and I reached for the pen. Helen, with sweetness and sadness and grace, said, "Let's try one with nothing in your hands."

The reason I'm in this little room today, MSNBC's Midtown Manhattan green room, is because twenty-four hours ago my life changed. I had spent nearly thirty years hiding from one word—the "s" word. You've already figured out the word. I've spent paragraphs avoiding the act of typing it. When you're young, you internalize that "stutter" is an ugly word. Everything about stutter is weird: those three t's, that "uh" in the middle that makes you think of "dumb." Stutter lands with a thud, like "gimp" or "retard." Your instinct is to run from stutter, to move the conversation away from stutter. Stutter is painful and awkward and something nobody wants to talk about.

Today is Friday, November 22, 2019. I'm here because yesterday I published an article in *The Atlantic* about the man who has become the most famous living stutterer, and I'm about to do something I've never considered doing: talk on TV. Just under twelve months from now, Joe Biden will be elected president of the United States. He somehow made it this far without tens of millions of people realizing not only that he stuttered as a young boy, but that he still stutters as an old man. There are dozens of writers at my publication who are more talented than me, more deserving than me, more qualified than me to interview the next president. I landed the assignment for the sole reason that I stutter, too.

You'd like to think that when these moments arise you stride toward them—chin up, chest out, triumphant horns blaring somewhere in the background. Right now I'm just scared. In ninety seconds I'll walk onto the set in a blue blazer with a transparent earpiece and a battery clipped to the back of my belt. I'll try to play the part of a person who's supposed to be there. But the moment I begin to speak, I know I'll make people uncomfortable. I have no idea how difficult these next fifteen minutes will be. And I have no idea what's waiting for me after that.

2

Dead Air

Nearly every decision in my life has been shaped by my struggle to speak. I've slinked away to the men's room rather than say my name during introductions. I've stayed home to eat silently in front of the TV rather than order off the menu at a Chinese restaurant. I've let the house phone, and my cell phone, and my work phone ring and ring and ring rather than pick up to say hello.

"... Huh ... huh ... huh ..."

I can never get through the "h."

It's the same sound you need to summon when your teacher takes attendance at the start of each school day. I've dreaded the confirmation of my presence in a physical space—"Here!"—because I know the black hole of the "h" will swallow the "ere."

I understand that my stutter may make you cringe, laugh, recoil. I know my stutter can feel like a waste of time—of yours, of mine—and that it has the power to embarrass both of us. And I've begun to realize that the only way to understand its power is to talk about it.

Since that morning I first stuttered on television, I've had profound conversations with stutterers from all over the world. I wanted to know how other people deal with it. Most of the time I just sat and listened, but I inevitably asked a version of the same question: How do you make peace with the shame of stuttering? What do you do with all the anger? The resentment? The fear? How do you accept an aspect of yourself that you're taught at such an early age to hate? I've also had some unexpected conversations with ghosts from my past. Now I'm trying to answer a few of the questions I've been asking others.

I'M STARING AT A MESSAGE from a stranger named Elizabeth.

"Hi—Although we haven't met . . ."

I almost delete it, but I keep reading. Elizabeth says she has just returned from Maine, where she happened to visit her son's kindergarten teacher, who at one point spoke glowingly about an article she'd read, written by a former student.

After a couple of back-and-forths, I suddenly have my kindergarten teacher's email address. Soon, I'll have her phone number. We make plans to talk, but now I'm too embarrassed to dial. *Why am I doing this? Why would she remember anything about me?* I tap out her number and nearly hang up.

Ms. Bickford says hello and her voice sounds exactly as it did twenty-seven years ago. She's loving and stern, soft-spoken and matter-of-fact. I recognize this voice as the narrator of countless childhood stories. I can see her holding a book, one thumb on the spine. She carefully rotates it so that I and the other cross-legged kids on the carpet can absorb the illustration before she turns the page. I feel calm when she reads. I enter a daze when she reads.

She was the first person to notice something was wrong with me.

"One of the things we used to do—I don't know if you

remember this—was something called 'Daily News,'" Ms. Bickford says.

As the phrase leaves her mouth, the tiniest of knots forms in my stomach.

Every day, when it was time for Daily News to begin, Ms. Bickford—she now goes by Mrs. Petty—would unfurl a chart of white paper at the front of the classroom. Each kindergartner was assigned a specific day of the week to come prepared with a piece of news to share.

"I would sit there and I would write, 'John said,' in quotation marks, and whatever sentence you would say, we would all read it back together," she reminds me.

I struggled with this activity from the start. At first, Ms. Bickford thought it was a memory issue. She proposed that the night before my news day I should peel a sticky note off my mom's yellow pad and draw a picture, a prompt, any sort of catalyst. I loved the Baltimore Orioles. I used to sketch asymmetrical baseballs with jagged little stitches coming off the hide.

Let's imagine my news: *Last night, my favorite player, Cal Ripken Jr., hit a big home run.* I'm standing at the front of the class. I have my sticky. I know the words. I *feel* the words. But I can't start the sentence and I don't know why. When I finally push the first word out, the second won't come.

"You didn't like that part of the day," she says. There's a twinge in her voice. Our nostalgic phone call has turned quiet. "You were just this sweet little guy with great curls."

My Daily News presentations never got easier. I soon hated being called on at all. Eventually, Ms. Bickford had a conversation with my mom: *Something is wrong. I think you should have him evaluated.*

. . .

WHEN MY SPEECH IMPEDIMENT appeared in the fall of 1992, stuttering was viewed as something to be fixed, solved, cured—and fast!—before it's too late. *You don't want your kid to grow up a stutterer.*

Only since around the turn of the millennium have scientists understood stuttering as a neurological disorder. But the research is still a bit of a mess. Few experts can even agree on the core stuttering "problem." Some people will tell you that stuttering has to do with the language element of speech (turning our thoughts into words), while others believe it's more of a motor-control issue (telling our muscles how to form the sounds that make up those words).

We start developing our ability to speak as babies. Our little coos and babbles are batting practice for future vowel and consonant sounds that will in time become sentences. Between 5 and 10 percent of all kids exhibit some form of disfluency. A child may speak without issue for the earliest years of his or her life, then, like me, start to stutter between the ages of two and five. For at least 75 percent of these kids, the issue won't follow them into adulthood. But with each passing year, it becomes harder and harder for a stutterer to speak fluently, or without interruption. If you still stutter at age ten, you're likely to stutter to some extent for the rest of your life.

It's helpful to think of "stuttering" as an umbrella term to describe a variety of hindrances in the course of saying a sentence. You probably know the classic stutter, that rapid-fire repetition: *I have a st-st-st-st-stutter.* But a stutter can also manifest as an unintended prolongation in the middle of a word: *Do you want to go to the moooooo-ooo-oovies?* Then there are blocks, which are harder to explain.

Blocking on a word yields a heavy, all-encompassing silence.

Dead air on the radio. You push at the first letter with everything you have, but seconds tick by and you can't produce a sound. The harder you force it, the more out of breath you become. The less breath you have to work with, the less likely it is that you'll move enough air through your lungs and larynx to say the word. Some blocks can go on for a minute or more. A bad block can make you feel like you're going to pass out. Blocking is like trying to push two positively charged magnets together: you get close, really close, and you think they're about to finally touch, but they never do. An immense pressure builds inside your chest. You gasp for air and start again. Remember: This is just *one word*. You may block on the next word, too.

We're told that three million Americans talk this way, but it doesn't feel that common. It's partly a hereditary phenomenon. A little over a decade ago, the geneticist Dennis Drayna identified three gene mutations related to stuttered speech. We now know there are at least four such "stuttering genes," and more are likely to emerge in the coming years. But even the genetic aspect is murky: stuttering isn't passed down from parent to offspring in a clear dominant or recessive pattern. Even when it comes to identical twins with identical genes, only one of them might stutter.

The average speech-language pathologist, or SLP, is taught to treat multiple disorders, from enunciation challenges (think of someone who has trouble articulating an "r" sound) to swallowing issues. Yet many therapists are ill-equipped to handle a multilayered problem like stuttering. Of the roughly 150,000 SLPs in the United States, fewer than 150 are board-certified stuttering specialists. Even today, there is strong debate within the medical community about how to effectively help a person with a stutter. Many teachers don't know how to deal with it either. It's lonely. You may have a sister or dad or grandparent who stutters, but in most cases, there's only one kid in class who stutters: *you.*

I WAS BORN IN Washington, D.C., and grew up in the leafy suburb of Takoma Park, Maryland. My mom was a nurse at Children's Hospital. She's one of seven kids, right in the middle, the compromiser, the peacekeeper.

She'd pick up my older brother, Matt, my only sibling, and me from school with off-brand sodas from Safeway waiting in the cupholders of our laurel blue Honda Accord. When we got home, she'd make me a grilled cheese on Pepperidge Farm bread. She'd walk into the TV room with the hot sandwich on a miniature cutting board in one hand, a bowl of potato chips in the other. She always had an endless stream of crumpled Kleenexes in her purse. (She'd hold a tissue to my nose and tell me to "put the fire out.") One Halloween I stood in the living room as she wrapped me head to toe in Ace bandages, turning me into a mummy. She used medical tape and pins from her nurse's kit to bind the disparate strands of first-aid material together. As she covered more and more of my body, she issued a dire warning: *If you have to pee, you better do it now.*

Ms. Bickford's news was hard for my mom to hear. She called our pediatrician, who referred her to a speech pathologist, who determined that I indeed had a problem but couldn't offer much in the way of help. We waited for a while, hoping it would get better on its own. It got worse. My next option was to see the multipurpose therapist in the little room at school.

My brother and I attended Holy Trinity, a Catholic elementary school in the city. My parents could afford it only because my mom cut a deal with the principal: she'd volunteer as the substitute nurse in exchange for discounted tuition. On the days she showed up at school for duty I'd head to the nurse's office in the basement and eat lunch with her on a laminated placemat. I loved those afternoons. But to get down there to see her, I had to walk past the little room. I hated that room. Every time I entered that room, I felt like a failure.

THERE'S THE KNOCK. Kids stare as I stand to leave class. I walk down two flights of slate steps, turn the corner, and enter the little room. Everything in the little room is little: little table, little chair, little bookshelf. But now I'm older and can hit a baseball and win Knockout at recess, so the decor is infantilizing. I've always been tall and gangly. At seven, my knees barely fit under the table. Most little rooms are peppered with the same five or ten motivational posters: neon block letters, emphatic italics, maybe an iceberg or some other visual metaphor to explain your complex existence. This little room has a strange brown carpet that I stare into when the school therapist brings up my problem. She's careful never to use the word "stutter."

Okay, let's start from the beginning.

There's a stack of books on the table that are meant for people younger than me. Most sentences in these books are composed of one-syllable words. The vowels on the page are emphasized—underlined or in bold—a visual cue for me to stretch out that sound. Today we're going to practice reading "car" as "cuuuuuhhhhhhhh-arrrrrrrr." This is embarrassing. I know what "car" sounds like. I know how other people say "car." Doing this exercise makes me feel like an idiot; not only is it hard to speak, but now it seems like I can't read. Every time I block on the "c," I sense a pinch of frustration from across the table. After enough attempts, I can read one whole sentence in a breathy, robotic monotone.

Thuuuhhhh cuuuuhhhh-aaarrrr drooooove faaaaaaast dowwwwwn thuuuuhhhhh rrroooaaaad.

For some reason, this way of speaking is considered a monumental success. I think the way I just read that is more embarrassing than my stutter. But I have to keep doing it, because it's the Big Rule: *Take your time.*

Have you ever told a stutterer to take their time? Next time you see them, ask how "take your time" feels. "Take your time" is a polite and loaded alternative to what you really mean, which is *Please stop stuttering.* Yet an alarming amount of speech therapy boils down to those three words.

After about forty minutes, I'm sent back to class. I exhale as I leave the little room. I climb the steps, crack the door, and shimmy back to my desk with a nervous smile. I roll my no. 2 Ticonderoga pencil between my thumb and index finger, scratching a fingernail against the metal part below the eraser, trying to release some of my frustration. I'm convinced everyone's wondering why I just walked out and returned a while later without explanation. I flip to a new page in my workbook and glance at the clock. I lower my head, praying not to be called on.

MS. BICKFORD HAS TAUGHT hundreds of students over the years. How did she remember all of those details about my stutter? Now I was wondering what others might remember. Roughly a month after our call, Ms. Bickford connected me with

Ms. Samson (now Mrs. Southern), my second-grade teacher, who later became my fourth-grade teacher. She's now in Colorado, raising three boys. She's still teaching.

"I love the fact that you're writing about this and putting it out there, because, gosh, from a teacher's point of view, there's not a lot, I mean, I wasn't trained . . ." She searched for the words. "I wasn't told how to handle this."

Holy Trinity was divided into an Upper School and a Lower School. The older kids had a cafeteria, but the younger kids ate lunch in their classrooms. Ms. Samson kept a little radio on the corner of her desk. At lunchtime, she'd tune in to WBIG Oldies 100, and the space in front of the whiteboard would become the second-grade dance floor. Each afternoon was like a kids' wedding reception, and every day I couldn't wait for it to start. I'd wolf down my turkey on white then push back my chair and dart to the front of the class. You knew that the station's midday DJ, Kathy Whiteside, had queued up a total hit parade: the Four Tops, the Supremes, the Temptations, Sam and Dave. This was an ideal time to work on your Running Man, or to whip out an invisible towel and do the Twist.

When Ms. Samson cranked her radio, my shoulders dropped and my lungs felt full. We looked like doofuses up there in our khaki pants and plaid skirts, but we were a *unit* of doofuses. This has special meaning when you're the class stutterer. An hour ago you were flustered and out of breath, pushing and pulling at a missing word, sensing that familiar sweat drip down the back of your neck. Now you're just another kid doing the swim to "Under the Boardwalk." One day you sashay over toward Michelle B. You giggle at each other. One afternoon you make eyes at each other. A new song starts. Jackie Wilson's voice lifts you higher and higher.

Then the music stops and you crash back to earth.

"Your face would turn blotchy. Really, really red," Ms. Samson told me. "You would cut your comments short because it was just too much work, or you figured, 'I lost the audience.' But your impulse to participate—that's how I knew: 'He's thinking. He's thinking and he wants to talk.' That was the hardest part."

This is the tension that stutterers live with: Is it better for me to speak and potentially embarrass myself or to shut down and say nothing at all? Neither approach yields happiness. As a young stutterer, you start to pick up little tricks to force out words. Specifically, you start moving other parts of your body when your speech breaks down.

I still do this, and I hate it. I don't know why it works, but it does: when I'm caught on a word, I can get through a jammed sound much faster if I wiggle my right foot. *Blocked on that "b"? Bounce your knee!* Unfortunately these secondary behaviors quickly become muscle memory. Sometimes they morph into tics. They also have diminishing returns: a subtle rub of your hands in January won't have the same conquering effect on a block in February. So that means you're stuttering for seconds at a time *and* moving other parts of your body like a weirdo. It's exhausting. The curse of these secondary behaviors is that they can be just as uncomfortable as your stutter.

In a few years you'll learn that other kids in your class have started talking on the phone at night. You can't imagine using the house phone without a pen in your hand to maniacally toss up and down as you attempt to call a girl's house. You pace around the TV room with the cordless phone wedged between your head and your right shoulder, one eye on the moving pen, trying to ask Michelle's brother Bryan if his sister is home. You can barely breathe. When he hands her the phone her greeting is soft and tragic: *Hi.* Now you're finally on the line and you don't have the energy to speak. Tomorrow you'll keep your head down and avoid her. You notice you start looking down a lot.

And there's that familiar knock. You rise from your desk and feel your classmates' eyes trail you. Down the stairs, around the corner, back to the little room. You've been coming down here for a while and you're not getting any better. You feel guilty for wasting everyone's time. A quiet voice in your head tells you it's all your fault. Soon your guilt starts to grow into a new emotion: shame. It can be hard to understand the difference between the two, but a friend who stutters once clarified it for me.

"Guilt is 'I *made* a mistake.' Shame is 'I *am* a mistake.'"

3

The Look

Okay, here comes our waiter.

I stare at the silverware.

He clicks his pen.

I'm always the last to order. Sometimes my mom tries to help me by tossing out what she thinks I want.

"Cheeseburger, John?"

". . . Yyyy-uhh . . . yyyueaah," I force out.

If I'm lucky there are no follow-up questions. I'm rarely lucky.

"And how would you like that cooked?" the waiter asks.

". . . . . Mmm-muh . . . . mmm-edium."

His face changes. I want it medium rare, but "r's" are hard, so I cut myself off.

"And what kind of cheese?"

Vowels are supposed to be easier, but I can never get through that first sound. I skip it altogether and go right for the consonant.

". . . Mmmmmuh . . . . . muhm-merican."

Now our waiter understands that something is wrong. He shoots a nervous glance at my mom, who fires back a strained smile: *Everything is fine. My son is fine.*

"Okay, next question," he says with stilted laughter. "Curly fries or regular?"

I want regular, but remember, "r's" are hard. Unfortunately "c's" are hard, too. I'm trapped. I try a last-second word switch. Bad idea.

". . . . Eeeeeeee-uh . . . . eeee-uh . . . . . . eeee-uh, eei-ther."

I close my menu and push it forward.

"And to drink?"

THE LOOK IS ALMOST ALWAYS the same. It's the moment the listener realizes something is wrong with you, that moment they subtly wince. They don't know whether to interject or to keep waiting while you try and fail to speak. They probably don't sense their shoulders rising and their head pulling away in discomfort. It's primal, this reaction: another body literally retreating from you, the problem. Even during the chaos of a stutter, you see it, all of it. The judgment. The pity. The *why does he talk like this?* expression. No matter how many years pass, no matter how numb you become, The Look never leaves you.

I've received The Look from parents, priests, schoolteachers, bosses, friends, and girlfriends. The Look stalked playgrounds when I was young and it was waiting for me behind the bar when I got older. Flight attendants and baristas and counter guys at the pizza place near my apartment throw me The Look. I get it from colleagues and neighbors and strangers at birthday parties. I don't blame them. You may have given someone The Look yourself, and I don't blame you. Odds are that you're part of the 99 percent of the population who don't stutter. But if you're among the 1 percent of people in the world who do, then I don't need to explain The Look to you. Someone gave you The Look earlier this morning. Someone else will give you The Look before you go to bed tonight.

The Look is one reason people who stutter look away.

Maybe you've noticed that stutterers drop their eyes when speaking. Some stutterers crane their neck up toward the ceiling, others stare into the middle distance, silently praying for the block to end. You leave your house, you attempt to speak, someone gives you The Look, and you turn away in self-defense. When you stutter you violate an unspoken deal: people talk this way, not that way. *Why are you talking like that? Stop talking like that.* Every time I start to stutter I feel a pang of sadness. There it is again. Another imperfect sentence. Another delay I'm adding to the conversation. Another time someone's gaze will drift from my eyes down to my mouth, where the car crash is happening.

In his influential 1956 work, *The Presentation of Self in Everyday Life,* the sociologist Erving Goffman argued that in every social interaction we are playing a part on an invisible stage. We want people to like us, to believe in us—no one wants to be labeled a fraud. Each time we speak, we may earn someone's respect or lose it. We strive to communicate in complete sentences without filler words ("um," "like," "you know") from elementary school up through adulthood. We go to great lengths to sound smart, because we know that strong communicators are deemed worthy of respect. Alex Trebek's peerless ability to enunciate phrases during his thirty-seven-year run on *Jeopardy!* transformed him into an icon. You can probably hear Trebek's voice in your head right now: the clarity, the dignity, the confidence, the poise. America loved Trebek because, among other things, he was very good at saying words.

Stutterers are often portrayed in pop culture as idiots, or liars, or simply incompetent. In the 1992 comedy *My Cousin Vinny,* people wince as the stuttering public defender blocks horribly throughout his opening statement. One juror drops his jaw in shock. (Austin Pendleton, a stuttering actor, played the part to an almost vaudevillian degree.) In Michael Bay's 2001 soapy blockbuster *Pearl Harbor,* crucial seconds are wasted on the morning of December 7, 1941, because Red, a soldier who stutters, can't speak under pressure. Red stumbles around the barracks gritting his teeth, trying to force out the news: "The JJJJ-JJJaps are here!" He eventually says it, but it's too late: enemy gunfire pierces the room where his friends are sleeping. Thanks to Red and his stupid stutter, more people than necessary have now died at Pearl Harbor.

A person who stutters spends their life racing against an internal clock.

How long have I been talking?

How long do I have until this person walks away?

When you're a kid, there's a quieter, slower, more insidious ticking:

Am I going to beat it before it's too late?

IN TIME, I STOPPED going to the little room and began seeing a new speech therapist once a week after school. Dr. Tommie Robinson worked out of a satellite facility on Sixteenth Street, not far from Children's Hospital. Each Wednesday he'd bound into the waiting room and greet me with a high five. He grew up in a big Mississippi family and spoke with a warm country drawl. He had an arsenal of crisp white shirts and silk ties. He oozed patience.

This arrangement was immediately better: No more leaving class, no more kids' books. Dr. Robinson's philosophy was to pair fluency-shaping strategies with things I'd encounter in my daily life, like board games. We tore through hours of Trouble, pressing down on the translucent dome to make the imprisoned die pop. As I moved my blue men around the board, I'd practice techniques to try to smooth out my speech. If we read passages out loud, we'd use my actual homework.

Dr. Robinson's go-to technique was a popular strategy called "easy onset." It's a spiritual cousin to "cuuuhhhh-aaaaarrrr," but with more emphasis on the first sound. The objective is to ease into the opening letter with a light touch, stretch the vowel, then shorten your exaggeration over time. No two stutterers struggle with the same collection of sounds, but every stutterer is haunted by specific vowels and consonant clusters. Many people who stutter come to dread the act of saying their own name. One reason for this is conditioning: we say our names more frequently than any other proper noun, and we tend to stutter most when we meet new people.

My jaw locks when I go to form the "j" in "John." I typically enter a long, painful block, then bark out the word at full volume: . . . . *JOHN!* Sometimes my "j" manifests as a rapid repetition, like a machine gun, or a Buick that won't start: *Jjjjjjjjjjjjjjjohn.* I've wasted whole afternoons fantasizing about what life might be like with another name. Why didn't my parents choose Michael? All I'd have to do is thread that "m" to the "i." The second syllable plops out, like a raindrop on a creek. *Michael.* I've said "Michael" so many times that it's lost all meaning: Michael, *Michael,* Miiiichael. (Of course, if I *were* Michael, I'd probably block on the "m.")

Stuttering is an invisible disability until the moment it manifests. To stutter is to live through hundreds of awful first impressions. And an awkward exchange between two people affects not just the person *being* awkward, but the person forced to deal with said awkwardness. A stutterer may enter a room full of "normal" people and temporarily pass as a fellow "normal," but the moment they open their mouth—the second that jagged speech hits another set of eyes and ears—it's over. As Goffman notes: "At such moments the individual whose presentation has been discredited may feel ashamed while the others present may feel hostile, and all the participants may come to feel ill at ease, nonplussed, out of countenance, embarrassed, experiencing the kind of anomy that is generated when the minute social system of face-to-face interaction breaks down."

One phrase leaps out at me there: "may feel ashamed." This assumes that the shame will pass. As you inch toward adolescence, the people around you become meaner, and the shame of having a stutter metastasizes. I wish I could pinpoint the moment that shame changed from something that periodically washed over me to something I lug around every day like a backpack.

DR. ROBINSON TRIED and failed to incorporate my brother into our early therapy sessions. Matt used to sit in the waiting room with my mom, between the fish tanks and the magazines, stewing until my appointment was over. Our car rides home frequently devolved into fights. Matt hated those Wednesdays, because Matt hated my stutter even more than I did.

My brother is one of the smartest, most hardworking people I have ever met. As a kid, he had a diverse portfolio of successful small businesses. He'd come down the hill with a wooden box of quarters after slinging Minute Maid concentrate lemonade at the top of our street. A neighbor hired him to walk her dog for three dollars a day and soon our neighborhood was littered with enticing blue flyers: "Need a Dog Walker? Call Matt!" For many summers, he awoke at dawn and took two buses several miles away to caddy at a country club, sometimes with one golf bag on each shoulder. He briefly hung around with the most interesting girl in his class, Claire, who introduced him to Nirvana, Pearl Jam, the Offspring, and other '90s bands I soon loved because—why else?—my brother loved them.

Matt also had a stutter, but his disappeared on its own when he was in kindergarten—in Ms. Bickford's class. ("He was a big personality," Ms. Bickford told me with a laugh.) He has a biting sense of humor. He loved *Seinfeld* and *Letterman* and would tape *Saturday Night Live* back when his classmates were still watching Nick at Nite.

My brother became adept at mocking my stutter. His was a full-body impersonation. He would flutter his eyes, scrunch his nose, and droop his mouth while pretending to be stuck on a word for seconds at a time. He'd push his head toward mine like a horse coming in for a carrot. He made awful sounds—my sounds—the sounds barnyard animals make on Fisher-Price toys. When he was mad, Matt used to remind me that he'd *beat* his stutter and that I hadn't, that I couldn't, that I never would.

SOME DAYS DR. ROBINSON and I would sit on the floor in front of the big mirror and study the movements of our mouths. This is harder than it sounds. You're back in the therapy room, working on strategies, but nothing is clicking. The mirror runs the length of the wall and there's nowhere else to look: you *have* to watch yourself stutter. If I sat close enough, with my eyes just a few inches away from the surface, I could make out shadowy figures in a dark room on the other side of it. The day I discovered this was a little like the year I learned the truth about Santa Claus: *You mean everyone knows but me?*

There was a hidden microphone somewhere in our room. The space on the other side had little speakers to transmit our voices. (You've seen this on a million cop shows.) One afternoon I asked Dr. Robinson who was in there watching us, and he told me: occasionally, graduate students observed our sessions, and that was a good thing, because we were teaching them how to be therapists themselves. Other days, the shadowy figure was my mom.

I DON'T BLAME HER for watching: that's what the doctors told her to do. I have sympathy for the parents of children who stutter. You want nothing more than for your kid to live a happy and successful life, and this new thing, this ugly problem, seems to threaten that. There's also the aforementioned race against time: with each passing year, the brain loses its plasticity, making true fluency harder to attain. Many health insurers don't cover speech therapy, preventing people with especially limited funds from having the chance to work with experts. And yet, even parents who have the means—those who dutifully shuttle their kids to appointments—often leave with problematic advice:

Remind them to use their techniques! Tell them to take their time!

We stutterers anticipate our blocks well before they occur. We know how our brains and lungs and lips confront every letter of the alphabet. We know what we look like, what we sound like, what we make shared spaces feel like. We know that our stutter hasn't gotten better, and that maybe it's getting worse. We sense that most nights you, Mom and Dad, pray for it to go away. We know you believe you're helping. We don't know how else to tell you this: you're not.

When a person of authority tells a young stutterer to "use your techniques," they are confirming the stutterer's worst fear: no one is listening to what you say, only how you say it. Enough of this makes you not want to talk at all. Fluency techniques may work in a therapy room, but, in most cases, they're extremely hard to deploy in the real world. Speaking like a robot is not natural. There's the voice in my head who reads this sentence, and a much different voice who reads it out loud. The two voices hate each other. They spend every day fighting for control, meaning neither is in control—I'm not in control.

"I could see you using strategies—you were doing things with your breath," Ms. Samson told me. "And probably you had practiced whatever it was so much, and just couldn't live up to what you knew you could do. I could see the defeat. You would put your head down and sort of walk back to your desk."

THE ASSIGNMENT WAS SIMPLE: Pick a parent and interview him or her about their job. I found my report buried in a box of old papers and photographs. It's 173 words, single-spaced. I typed it on my dad's IBM word processor. Early handwritten drafts are stapled to the back so that I could track the story's progress. At the end of the packet are two narrow sheets of yellow paper, ripped from a reporter's notebook. I wrote my dad's answers in chicken scratch and drew horizontal lines between each one—something I still do when interviewing people today.

JOHN HENDRICKSON

4th Grade

October 2, 1997

Has your dad ever been on the road with the Orioles? Well, mine has. Paul Hendrickson is an author, a reporter, a feature story writer, and he's also my dad.

Paul said that his favorite feature story was called "Driving Ms. Fannie." He told me that it appeared on the front page of The Washington Post. It was about driving a homeless woman back to Tennessee to see her family. She hadn't seen her brother in 40 years.

Paul told me that reporting is more fun than writing because you find out what makes the world tick. Maybe someday I'll be an author, a reporter, a feature story writer, and a dad.

I loved going with my dad into the old *Washington Post* building on Fifteenth and L. It had an omnipresent murmur, a classic newsroom buzz. I'd wander through the gray cubicle maze amid rumbling file cabinets, ringing desk phones, and pattering keyboards. Everyone seemed to know what was happening a full day before it happened. Over by the elevators was a black-and-white portrait of Cool "Disco" Dan, the photo that accompanied my dad's 1991 profile of the infamous D.C. graffiti artist. Many of my classmates' parents were lawyers or doctors, and most of those families had more money than we did, but my dad had a stack of press badges from faraway places.

I tagged along with him on a few reporting trips. One Saturday night we went to a rodeo in New Jersey and I watched as he wandered the grounds and interviewed bull riders. I shook hands with a cowboy who had little nubs instead of fingers. I'll never forget the way his hand felt in mine, how I tried hard to play it cool when meeting this person with a strange difference.

On the drive home I felt depressed: *Is that what people have to do when they meet me?*

I loved journalism because it seemed like so much fun, because every day seemed different. Plus, there was the payoff: some mornings when the *Post* showed up on our doorstep my dad's name would be in it. Yet as much as I dreamed of a future as a professional writer, I struggled to silence that little voice: *No one will hire you if you're a stutterer. How are you even going to ask people questions?*

My dad was frequently on the road, and when he wasn't traveling he would come home late. My mom and I would often pick him up from the Takoma Metro station well after dark. She'd sit next to him at the dining room table as he ate a slab of meat loaf or a plain hamburger with ketchup. My brother was upstairs, or somewhere else. I used to joke that I often ate dinner with my other family, *The Simpsons*.

For years, a few classmates and I would come to school the next morning and repeat dialogue from the previous night's back-to-back episodes. "Don't make me run, I'm full of chocolate!" "Aurora borealis? At this time of year? At this time of day?" "Back to the hammocks, my friend!" I would stutter as I said these lines, but we'd be laughing so hard that it wouldn't matter. Nothing shaped my understanding of culture, of humor, of life more than my nightly *Simpsons* dinner. At 5:59, I'd close my textbook and race to the TV room. I'd sit alone on the corduroy two-seater couch and eat a bowl of angel hair pasta with a glob of Prego, enthralled. On a commercial break I'd bring my empty bowl out to the sink, where my mom would often be wandering back and forth across the kitchen on the cream-colored phone with the long coiled cord, talking to one of her sisters in Pennsylvania. She'd wash the dishes after doing all the cooking. She'd dry the dishes, put the pots away, then gather all of our laundry and lug it downstairs. She'd place the basket on the chipped and dented ping-pong table—wash, dry, fold, lug. What were the rest of us even doing while she was handling all of this?

Ms. Samson came to know almost all of her students' families intimately. When I was in fourth grade, Matt was in eighth, on the verge of entering high school. As a young teenager, Matt started attacking both me and my stutter more aggressively. His teasing turned into bullying. Then his bullying became something else. Ms. Samson later told me that my mom confided in her about my brother's behavior toward me.

"She was seeing something that was getting out of control, and she didn't know what to do about it," Ms. Samson said. "She didn't talk at length, but she just wanted to give me the input of this is what you were dealing with, that home life was not necessarily a great place for you."

4

Balls and Strikes

On Sunday, September 20, 1998, Cal Ripken Jr. removed himself from the Baltimore Orioles' starting lineup against the New York Yankees. The next morning, *The Washington Post* published a photograph of Ripken sitting on the bench, looking wholly out of his element. The picture ran beneath a mammoth, wordless headline: "2,632." That was the number of consecutive games Ripken had played without taking a day off. A few seasons earlier, he had broken Lou Gehrig's previous record of 2,130 games. "The streak almost ended several times when Ripken suffered injuries to his back, knee or ankle," *Post* sportswriter Richard Justice wrote. "But each time, he made it back on the field."

I was ten years old when Cal sat down. I cut the strip of newspaper out, trimmed the edges, and glued it to a piece of black construction paper. Later that night, my dad helped me slide it into an old wooden picture frame. I brought the image to school the next day and hung it on the coat hook in the back of my locker. It's now resting on the bookshelf behind my desk. Ripken was a poetic infielder, a clutch hitter, a nineteen-time All-Star, but none of those things made him my hero. I idolized Cal because he kept showing up.

We were a baseball family. My dad and I would play catch on

warm mornings before school. My brother and I played hours of Wiffle ball and Home Run Derby with various babysitters, until Matt inevitably mocked my stutter or pegged me with the ball and I went inside. Each year my dad would drive us to Camden Yards for an Orioles game or two. We'd park at a gas station and buy dollar hot dogs outside the Eutaw Street gates under the B&O Warehouse. We never had great seats. It didn't matter. We were there. Cal was there.

My childhood bedroom was covered in blue pinstripe wallpaper, like a baseball uniform. I hung two posters over my bed: a photo of Ripken's curtain call from the night he broke Gehrig's record, and a sepia-tone image of a stoic Jackie Robinson. Above Ripken's outstretched arm was the word "PERSEVERANCE," with a definition of "persevere" on the bottom: "1. To continue a course of action, in spite of difficulty, opposition, or discouragement. 2. Remain steadfast." The Jackie Robinson poster was more direct: "COURAGE—1. The mental or moral strength to venture, persevere, and withstand danger, fear, or difficulty. 2. Valor."

Those images were the last thing I saw each morning before I went downstairs for a Pop-Tart or an Eggo waffle breakfast. Then I'd climb into the backseat and wonder how long I could go before my speech would fail again.

THE UPPER SCHOOL lunchroom consisted of rows of tables in a cramped basement with low ceilings, the type of space where sound echoes. One afternoon, a newer kid in class, Kenny, turned around, flared his eyes, and broke into a loud, fake stutter while others in the cafeteria watched: *"J-J-J-J-J-J-J-JOHNNNNN!"*

My best friend, Andrew, brought it up recently. I've known Andrew since I was three years old. As fourth graders we stood shirtless in front of his bathroom mirror sizing up each other's incoming armpit hair. As thirteen-year-olds, we sat on the floor in front of his TV, pausing and rewinding a particular scene from *American Pie*. I watched Andrew eat the exact same sandwich—peanut butter and jelly on soggy Wonder bread—almost every day for eleven years.

"I always felt bad, because I was sitting with Kenny when that happened, and I felt associated with that," he told me. Andrew remembered how another friend of ours, Danny, stepped in and defended me that day. His voice cracked as he told the story. "You don't do that type of thing," he said.

The truth is, stutterers come to expect these sorts of random attacks from their peers. One minute you're among a dozen guys playing touch football on a stretch of muddy grass, and the next, a classmate is charging at you, fake stuttering in your face after a big play. You try to laugh it off or pretend like it's not happening. You never want to talk about it.

Andrew lived in an old brick town house with curved banisters and leaning staircases. There was a guest room next to his bedroom that his mom used to call "John's room" because I slept over so often. I loved how I could open the window and listen to taxis drive by at night.

When I'd go to someone's house and everyone ate dinner together, I felt like Jane Goodall studying another species. Andrew's dad would hold court at the head of the table. He'd recite an interesting fact from the paper, then ask us what we learned that day.

"I don't know if you ever noticed this, but sometimes, if you were struggling with a word at dinner, my mom would try to tap on the table to a beat, thinking that that would help you," Andrew said.

Knowingly or not, she was taking a guerrilla approach to something called syllable-timed speech, or STS. This is another fluency-shaping method that therapists sometimes suggest for young stutterers. The goal is to ignore the natural rhythms of conversation and enunciate every word of each sentence one syllable at a time. Supporters of STS believe it can effectively retrain the brain and manufacture fluency where there is none; opponents argue that STS yields nothing more than the same forced robot talk.

"My mom would go on about your stutter to me," Andrew said. *"Is it getting better? Is it getting worse? Has he tried this? Has he tried that?"*

We tried everything.

At the suggestion of Sister Regina, a Holy Trinity nun, I even saw a hypnotist. Once a week for a couple of months my mom would drive me to this strange man's house and I'd descend to his dark basement. He'd hook me up to an array of wires and instruments to measure my heart rate and breathing patterns. I'd close my eyes and he would talk to me in a calming voice, then try to get me to speak that way back to him. He recorded every session on blank cassette tapes and instructed me to listen back to the sound of my momentarily smooth speech every night as I drifted off to sleep and . . . *voilà!*

It didn't work.

Andrew pointed out that, before this conversation as adults, he and I had never really talked about my stutter at all. He asked if I remembered my page in our big class project at the end of fifth grade. He still had his copy of the laminated blue book; I hadn't seen or thought about mine in decades. I later found it buried in a box of homework that my mom had set aside in our basement. Each page of the book features a grainy portrait and a miniature biography. In my photo, I'm half smiling with a huge gap between my two front teeth. A dark shadow streaks across the right side of my face. As I'm staring at the page now, I'm struck by what my classmate Lindsay wrote about me:

> John is happy with himself overall, but he thinks there are some things he could do better. If John could change one thing about his life, it would be his stuttering. It keeps him from doing things like reading in church.
>
> For the future, John wants to be a baseball player. He is inspired by his older brother, Matt, Cal Ripken and Jackie Robinson. If he can't play, he'd like to be a sports writer. If not that, he'd like to be an actor, someone like the next Tom Hanks.

I had to stop and reread that last line. That a stutterer would dream of becoming an actor sounds counterintuitive, but it's oddly logical. Ms. Samson told me that I would change before her eyes when performing skits in class: "The amount of joy you had on your face—it was unbelievable," she said. "You just didn't get moments like that often."

Humans rely on a different part of the brain for recitation than we do for impromptu conversation, and thus we use different neural pathways to communicate memorized speech. When you step onstage, you immediately become someone else. Julia Roberts, Nicole Kidman, and Harvey Keitel have all dealt with stutters; Jimmy Stewart and Marilyn Monroe stuttered long before them. For years, Emily Blunt has used her celebrity platform to bring attention to the disorder. She always encourages young stutterers to try their hand at drama.

"Honestly, John, I don't even know how it really happens,"

she told me. "It was quite miraculous for me." She was film-ing a TV show in her native England when we spoke. Blunt comes from an extended family of stutterers. As a young girl, she would hide her head and contort her limbs when pushing through severe blocks. "It was like an imposter in my body," she said. "I felt pissed about it. I was fucking furious about it."

In middle school, a teacher encouraged her to try out for a play. "He said, 'I've seen you do those accents and voices—why don't you just do it in a silly voice and give it a go?'" She turned on what she describes as a "dreadful" Northern English accent, and, to her amazement, she was fluent. Most audiences have no idea that Blunt *ever* struggled to speak or that, all these years later, she still lives with bits of her old stutter.

"As I was speaking to you just then, I know the words that I was tripping on—a word like 'forever.' That sound is hard for me. I'm aware of it talking to you, because we're talking about it. I think there are subliminal verbal gymnastics going on all the time that I have been doing since I was a kid to get over the hesitations," she said.

Alex Brightman, a Broadway actor, still manages his disflu-ency onstage.

"I never say, 'I'm an actor who stutters,'" he told me. "Not because I'm not proud of it, and not because it's something that I am ashamed of, it's just not the thing I'm advertising."

He laughed with a mix of embarrassment and affection as he told the story of the first musical that moved him as a child. (It was *Cats*.) He was eight years old when he took his seat in the mezzanine of the Winter Garden Theatre, just north of Times Square. Alex and his family were visiting New York from their home in Northern California. As the house lights went down and the curtain rose, he felt electric. His stutter could get so bad that he would fake being sick, trudge to the nurse's office, call home, and dive headfirst into the backseat of his mom's car, sobbing. But now he was three thousand miles away from all of that. None of it mattered. He was sitting in the dark in a Broadway audience, rapt. Some twenty-one years later, he took an opening-night bow on the same Winter Garden stage. He even received Tony nominations for his lead performances in the Broadway versions of *Beetlejuice* and *School of Rock*.

Brightman can talk for hours about the way drama changed his life and how the mechanics of performance can unlock something in a young stutterer.

"There are things that I do vocally and breathwise and pausewise that if I were to make you aware of them—and you probably are keenly aware—but others, when I tip them off to it, they can all of a sudden see through the matrix of what I'm doing," he said. He speaks in spurts, constantly raising and lowering his voice, curling around words. He's like a cartoon character come to life. "There is a bit of a calculation running in the background here, like another program that keeps me fluid."

He was bullied at school. "I tried to fight, I was tiny, it didn't work." So trying to make people laugh was the next best option. He's now in his thirties, and his comedic timing is flawless. But it's not just jokes: Brightman's vocal delivery is so deft that, as with Blunt, nonstutterers would likely never notice that he ever struggles. He can still feel the stutter inside of him, and it occasionally returns during moments of stress.

For his title role in *Beetlejuice,* Brightman found a gravelly and scratchy voice, like a chain-smoking Popeye. Nearly every stutterer I know has gone through a phase when they've turned on a new speaking voice as they search for fluency. For about two weeks in elementary school, if I was struggling with a word, I adopted an alien growl. I have no idea where this voice came from. I can still see my neighbor Nick holding a basketball and looking at me dumbfounded as I broke into a high-pitched impression of Louis Armstrong while we played Horse.

But unlike some stutterers, drama never cured me in the long run. During our school play about the Harlem Renaissance, every kid had a part, and I had exactly one line. It came at the end of a monologue in which classmates would speak from different parts of the stage. I was responsible for three words: "Place. Sound. Celebration." There were even built-in pauses between each word. I blocked horribly during rehearsals, dropping and jerking my head, spasming in the empty theater. The director mercifully gave the first and third words to someone else; now all I had to say was one word in the middle: "Sound."

One syllable.

Five letters.

C'mon, you can do this.

"..... Sss ...... sssssss ..... ssss .... sssssssssssssss ..."

I couldn't do it.

I eventually asked the director to give away *that* line, my solitary word, to someone else. I was the only person in the show who didn't speak.

I'VE SPENT MY LIFE dreading the phone, hiding from it, yet somehow I called Julie Brandenburg almost every night during the 1999–2000 school year. What did we even talk about? I would close the door to the TV room and sit on the radiator as MTV flickered in the background. Half an hour would go by, then forty-five minutes, then an hour, then ninety minutes. My right ear would get warm from cradling the receiver. No matter what had happened that day at school, or however badly my brother was treating me at home, Julie helped me escape. I could stutter on the phone with her and it wouldn't matter.

She's now Julie McGaffin, happily married and a mother of two, living in Maryland.

"John?"

Her voice is a time machine. (Yes, it is hilariously weird to interview your sixth-grade girlfriend.)

Julie has deep brown eyes and a smile that takes up half her face when she lets it. On middle school field trips, Julie and I idled next to each other. We jumped on the huge trampoline in her backyard and went sledding at the high school near her house. One night we went roller-skating at Jelleff, the Boys & Girls Club behind the Safeway. We held sweaty hands for shaky laps around the rink as Britney Spears and the Backstreet Boys sang about love.

"I always knew in my gut that this wasn't something that could have been easy to live with," Julie told me. "You just carried yourself—and maybe it was because you didn't have any other option—you just made it seem like you weren't hurting at all."

That was my only strategy during those years: Suppress it. Ignore it. Never talk about it. Don't let the bad feelings come to the surface. It worked for a while, until it didn't.

Julie's dad loved baseball just as much as I did. Shortly before she came to our school in fourth grade, her father was diagnosed with ear, nose, and throat cancer. He underwent surgery that left his lips in a perpetually pursed state, and it was often hard to understand him. "Marbles in his mouth," as Julie put it. Still, I loved talking to him, and he always made me feel whole. He could convey so much emotion through the upper part of his face.

"I felt very bad for my dad," Julie said. "He was, you know, a fifty-seven-year-old man who was having to learn how to communicate all over again, and he was embarrassed. He hated it. It felt really nice to have someone in our life who was going through something that I felt at the time could be compared, you know? You were a teacher for me."

One night Julie and I snuck up to the third floor of the Lower School and became each other's first kiss. We half joked about getting married. Then one day it appeared: the dreaded piece of torn notebook paper, folded seven or eight times, bubble text, purple ink. *I'm very sorry. I have a new crush.*

After the pain wore off, Julie and I remained good friends, and she even came to watch me play baseball. A year later we were in the same small writing class. As much as I dreaded having to read my stories out loud, I loved the clarity and control that came with composition. Julie noticed. "It was one of those moments, even as a kid, where I was like, 'Holy crap, this may be what he does forever.'"

I asked Julie if we ever talked about my brother during all those nights we spent on the phone.

"I always thought that Matt was like . . . this ghost," she said.

ANDREW SAW MORE SIDES of my family than anyone else. He was there in the backseat when I stuttered as I proudly told my dad I had made the all-star baseball team. ("Your brother turned around and, without any congratulations from anyone else in the car yet, said, 'They just gave that to you because they felt sorry for you.'") If I was caught in a really bad block, Matt would hold up his hand and say, "Not interested," then walk away. If my brother had friends coming over, he might warn me not to talk.

My brother is a big guy, and by his sophomore year of high school he was already taller and stronger than my dad. A lot of these nights blur together, but certain images stand out. There was an old Rand McNally atlas that my dad used to mark up state by state, page by page, a totem he had taken on dozens of reporting trips. One night Matt tore it to pieces in front of his face. Another night he grabbed the radio that my dad kept on his bookshelf to listen to Orioles games, then smashed it on the walkway outside our house.

Many families know these patterns. When you're a kid growing up in a home with periodic violent outbursts, you pick up little details about how the world works. Screaming back in someone's face only makes the situation worse. Guys who say they're about to throw a punch don't really *want* to punch.

I LOST A LOT OF SLEEP on a lot of school nights. There were nights when my mom would race to the kitchen phone, threatening to call the cops as my brother tore through the house after something set him off.

One night I threw a change of clothes and my toothbrush in my backpack and rushed to meet my mom in the car. Suddenly we were driving up the street, crying, catching our breath, and checking into the Motel 6 on Georgia Avenue. When we went home the next day, there was no real plan to make it stop, and as these years passed, my stutter kept getting worse.

The Fluency Factory

I felt guilty that I had been going to speech therapy for years and had nothing to show for it. An uncomfortable option was looming in the distance in Roanoke, Virginia: Hollins. The full and proper name is the Hollins Communications Research Institute, but to stutterers, it's just Hollins.

Its website is an enticing corner of the internet—not least because of its all-encompassing domain, stuttering.org. The before-and-after videos are shocking: Here's Alexandra, cheeks puffed, eyes pinched, chin bouncing. She's struggling to say her name. And here's Alexandra, some days later, speaking into the camera with a tranquil gaze and syrupy smoothness. She seems at peace. How could any stutterer say no?

I guess I didn't want to believe that my problem was so bad that it required hundreds of miles of travel, thousands of dollars in fees, and an extended stay in a hotel for the simple task of trying to speak in an artificial way I'd probably hate. Then there was the other question: What if it didn't work?

IN THE FALL OF 1966, Anne Oberhelman was sitting in her freshman biology class at Hollins University when a visitor appeared. He introduced himself as Dr. Ron Webster, a member of the school's psychology department. A few years earlier, while pursuing his Ph.D. at Louisiana State, Dr. Webster had researched the sounds that babies make as they first begin to speak. He exposed infants to a range of verbal stimulation—some of it rich with vowels, some heavy on consonants. Working with a speech pathologist, he transcribed their sounds phonetically and classified them. This led to a question: Why do certain babies grow up to speak abnormally? At Hollins, a women's college, he was working on a new project, zeroing in on those who stutter. Oberhelman stopped him after class: "Dr. Webster, I *have* to be involved in this."

Oberhelman's high school boyfriend (and eventual husband), Bill, was a stutterer. If he called her house and one of her family members answered, he would hang up. Bill's disfluency made him miserable; he often avoided speaking at all. He couldn't even bring himself to say the word "stutter." His best friend prodded him: *Come on, Bill, you can tell me, you can talk about it.* Nope. Nor would he confide in Oberhelman. She was desperate to help him.

Dr. Webster approached stuttering from a deceptively simple starting point: people don't stutter when they sing. This is almost universally true. Elvis Presley, Bill Withers, Carly Simon, and Oasis's Noel Gallagher are just a few of the names on the long list of singers who have dealt with stutters. As a young stutterer, Ed Sheeran would rap along with Eminem's *The Marshall Mathers LP,* something he credits with helping him find fluency. Kendrick Lamar was a stutterer long before he became the greatest living rapper, and he believes his childhood stutter is one of the reasons he poured his energy into making music.

I *never* stutter when I sing. I never even worry about the *prospect* of stuttering when I sing. Songs are built on melody and rhythm, with specific moments that tell us when to pause for a new breath: "Country rooaaaddsssss [breath], take me hoooommeeeee [breath]." In many cases, a person has memorized the song's lyrics, or an approximation of them. When you sing along with the radio, you're joining another voice, so the choral element alleviates some of the performance pressure. This also applies to recitation, or what researchers call "choral speech." As a kid, I could stand and recite the Pledge of Allegiance with the rest of my classmates, all thirty little voices in high-pitched unison, and I would never stutter. But if I was asked to take the lead before others joined in—"I pledge allegiance . . ."—I would block hard on that first "I." This led to a painful question: "Why do you speak normally sometimes but not all the time?" I never had an answer.

The process of converting thoughts into consonant and vowel sounds and then voicing them happens on the scale of tens of milliseconds. Dr. Webster theorized that stuttering could be cured by retraining certain speech muscles, like the ones around the lungs and throat. His first participants came from a range of backgrounds, though many were men in their twenties, thirties, and forties. Some of them had violent secondary behaviors; one man swung his head at a ninety-degree angle six, seven, or eight times in succession as he tried to wrestle out a word. Half a century later, Oberhelman's voice still tenses up when describing the scenes that she saw as an undergraduate researcher.

"Whenever I hear a stutterer have a block, it's like they have an open wound, and I can't put pressure to stop the bleeding," Oberhelman told me. "I have to just let it clot by itself—that's what it feels like."

"Does it . . . sound like that now . . . on the phone with me?" I asked.

"Um, yeah, a little bit."

VIRGINIA PSYCHOLOGIST TREATS STUTTERERS
BY COMPUTER-ASSISTED THERAPY,
BUT SOME EXPERTS VOICE DOUBT

That was the headline in the March 27, 1972, edition of *The New York Times*. The story ran on the same page as a small ad for Jim Bailey's nightly shows at the Copacabana.

During those early sessions, each stutterer was presented with a copy of *Reader's Digest* and a set of headphones. The stutterers would read aloud while the researchers pumped white noise into their ears, making it nearly impossible for participants to hear their own disfluency. (At the time, Dr. Webster was also working under an incorrect assumption that stuttering may be tied to a middle-ear issue.)

Oberhelman would sit with the participants and tally their repetitions, blocks, and prolongations—both with and without the auditory aid. The white noise appeared to help distract participants from their stutter, but only briefly. With a little practice, many stutterers were able to slow down the rate of their speech and speak fluently in a controlled, closed environment, but their stutter would roar back when they picked up the telephone or spoke in public. Dr. Webster was undeterred. He was convinced he could fully reconstruct stuttered speech.

The Hollins Communications Research Institute claims that 93 percent of its clients achieve fluency by the end of treatment, and of that group, 75 percent are able to maintain fluency two years later. Those are amazing stats, though the math is curious. Since its inception, Hollins has treated more than 7,000 stutterers. Those impressive percentages, 93 and 75, are not derived from all 7,000 alumni who have passed through the program; they refer to a much smaller pool of individuals who voluntarily choose to share their progress with Hollins.

What about everyone else?

Chris Cochran, a communications director at Adidas, went through Hollins twice—first in middle school, then again as a junior in college. Each time he was able to manufacture temporary fluency, and each time his stutter returned in the weeks that followed. His lack of progress was defeating, not least on account of his family's investment: Hollins's twelve-day intensive program currently costs $4,285.

When Dr. Webster and I first spoke, in the fall of 2020, I told him that I had heard many stories of this nature from other stutterers.

He bristled. "Yeah, it's the real world that we live in, isn't it?"

I asked him how my disfluency compares with that of his average client.

"I would say that you're probably around, uh, a little more than moderate severity, with excursions into greater levels of severity," he said. "You seem to miss a lot of initial articulatory positions. You're in the wrong place to make the sounds you intend to make, but you've got the wrong forces, and the wrong vocal track shapes."

I told him that most of my stuttering involved blocks. "Occasionally, I'll have repetitions, um, namely on the word, uh, 'st-st-st-stutter,'" I said.

"What does that mean to you?" he asked.

I was thrown off by his question.

"It, um, it's a—it's a breakdown in the neural pathway from brain to lungs and voice box and mouth, you know, that whole journey, it's—"

"Let me interrupt. What is happening in your larynx?"

I told him that I had never heard of a speech therapist interrupting a stutterer.

DR. SCOTT YARUSS is a professor of communicative science and disorders at Michigan State University. He's spent years studying variability in speech patterns.

"I know countless people who have told me, 'Oh yeah, Hollins works great for me, I've been three times'—which is in and of itself an oxymoron," he said. "My own caseload has been quite filled over the decades with people who've previously achieved fluency through artificial speech means, who've tried it, who couldn't keep it, who crashed and burned." He noted that stutterers who glimpse temporary fluency and later lose it may come away with lower self-esteem than they had before. Dr. Yaruss and his colleagues have a phrase for Hollins and other programs like it: "chasing the fluency god."

"Maybe with age comes a little bit more frankness, but I personally believe those types of promises to be harmful," he said. "And I'd say it right to Ron's face, although I don't know that he'd talk to me."

Dr. Yaruss is among the more progressive bloc of therapists who focus on helping stutterers manage their adverse reactions to the sensation and dread of stuttering, rather than instruct them to smooth everything out first and feel better about themselves after.

"Society is judging them, saying stupid things to them, like 'What, you forget your name?' and talking over them, and holding up fluency as a goal," he said of his patients. "I've seen people's lives change in a weekend, literally, and it's not because they spent thousands and thousands of dollars to go to a weekend Hollins type of therapy. It's because they met other people who cared about them, who didn't care about the fluency of their speech but the content of what they were saying, and expressed to them that total acceptance."

Chris Cochran, the stutterer who went through Hollins twice, told me that he began to find peace with his stutter only in his twenties, when he accepted that it probably wasn't going to change. After years of keeping everything in, he now regularly talks about his problem with a close circle of friends and family members, particularly his wife, Erin.

"She sees me for the man who I see and who I want to be—she sees me as a person," he said. "For a long time, I never wanted kids, because of the genetic aspect of passing on my speech. And it was Erin who said, 'Hey, if they stutter, they couldn't have a better teacher to help them come to terms with it.'"

In the end, I never tried Hollins. Even though some famous stutterers, like the newscaster John Stossel, claim it changed their life for the better, I was nervous that it would change mine for the worse. Because however much I dreaded stuttering, I was even more afraid of adopting artificial-sounding speech. I'm not alone. In my conversation with Dr. Webster, I told him that the more time I spent researching stuttering as an adult, the more skepticism I was encountering about the efficacy of fluency-shaping programs like Hollins, as a whole.

"If you talk about speech reconstruction the way we do, the details we work with, we think we're on the right track," he said. "But we've got more to learn, absolutely, and so do all these other people."

He bristled once more.

"It's pretty easy to be a critic. It's very hard to stand up, pull up your socks, and make some progress in the real world."

6

Hard to Explain

I was thirteen years old when the Strokes' debut album, *Is This It,* took over the world. I loved it, but I was baffled by it. Why are their guitars so fuzzy? How does he do that to his voice? Where do you even get pants like that? I'd walk through the halls of Holy Trinity in my dumb uniform humming "Last Nite" and "Hard to Explain." At night I'd try to make lead singer Julian Casablancas's pouty face in my bedroom mirror. My aunt Nancy gave me a subscription to *SPIN* for Christmas that year. The day it arrived in the mail, I'd read it cover to cover, dog-earing pages to reread the next day. This was 2001—an amazing time to be an eighth-grade music nerd. Over the summer, my dad had taken me to see U2 at the MCI Center. It was a quasi-religious experience. We stood in the nosebleeds and I swayed along to every song, blissfully anonymous alongside twenty thousand other fans, feeling like I was leaving my body. Bono sprinted around the heart-shaped stage as I screamed the lyrics to "Pride" and "Sunday Bloody Sunday," never stuttering once. I felt free.

Is This It came out the month after 9/11. Holy Trinity is across the Potomac River from the Pentagon, about a ten-minute drive from where American Airlines Flight 77 crashed. That day, around ten a.m., a few minutes into third period, an administrator rushed in and whispered something to our art teacher about an attack. Mrs. Crowley, our principal, dismissed everyone at ten thirty. My dad was out of town and my mom couldn't get there right away, so she relayed a message to the receptionist: *Tell John to go with Andrew.* As we grabbed our backpacks and started to leave, we saw the Schafer twins, Katie and Erika, crying on a couch near the exit. Their father worked at the Pentagon. (They later learned he was okay.)

D.C. was eerily quiet. Andrew and I walked by a pizza place filled with strangers staring up at a wall-mounted TV with their mouths open. When we reached his house we pushed open his front door and sprinted to the third floor. Andrew pulled the collapsible ladder down from the bathroom ceiling. We climbed to the roof and gazed out at the thick cloud of black smoke rising from the Pentagon. The plume looked like nothing we'd ever seen, save for grainy images of Hiroshima.

School was canceled the next day. When we went back on Thursday, our English teacher, Ms. Celano, instructed us to pull out a piece of paper and write without stopping. We did that almost every day that year. My stutter had been getting worse as I moved through puberty, but little stories and essays were pouring out of me during these free writes. Ms. Celano never graded them. More than anything, they were therapeutic. I needed this.

THE BLACK-AND-YELLOW For Sale sign appeared on our front lawn in the spring of 2002. A few years earlier, my dad had left the *Post* for a teaching job at the University of Pennsylvania. He had been staying in a spare room in a house outside Philadelphia, riding Amtrak up and down the East Coast each week. My parents had talked about moving for a while, but this sign made it official: we'd be relocating to Pennsylvania when the school year ended. I was devastated.

I slept at Andrew's house a lot that year, even on occasional weeknights. After school we'd play hours of pickup basketball at Rose Park with his little brother, Will, tagging along behind us. We'd stay up late listening to WHFS, the local alt-rock station. We'd talk about high school and my impending move. As with Julie, I'd stutter like hell, but it temporarily wouldn't matter. Andrew never once made me feel like I was embarrassing him.

"I couldn't envision you and Matt ever, like, hanging out at home," he later told me. "I just knew it was a different relationship than me and Will."

My parents never had a college fund for my brother and me, but now that my dad had this teaching job, their finances were starting to come together. Matt had good grades and high SATs and was on his way to Penn with my dad's tuition discount. "Everything will be easier" was the message I kept hearing. Nonetheless, all along I was waiting for something to swoop in and cancel the whole move. One morning on the way to school I asked my mom if she and I could stay in D.C. and live in an apartment together. She cried.

The moving trucks showed up in the middle of June, two weeks after I finished eighth grade. I remember turning onto our new street a few miles outside of Philadelphia with the strange sensation that it was just a random street, not *my* street. The new house had an attic that my parents let me claim as my room. It was stuffy and dark in the summer and had no heat in the winter, but it was a great place to waste days. I spent most of those first few months ripping pages out of *SPIN* and *Rolling Stone* and thumbtacking them to the walls, trying to cover every inch of white space. I amassed an array of tattered rugs and old chairs from secondhand stores and yard sales. My dad helped me put an old door on top of two file cabinets and turn it into a desk. I'd sit up there all night listening to CDs, dreading September.

FIRST DAY OF HIGH SCHOOL, 2002. An alphabetical seating chart and an "H" last name places me in the middle of the class, third row, last seat. The wave of introductions starts in the corner. It makes its way through the first row, one student at a time. My eyes dart from each classmate telling us their name, hometown, and an interesting fact to the clock on the wall above the black-and-purple Believe to Achieve poster. I try to steady my breathing. I clench my fingers into tight fists. My right knee bounces uncontrollably. Now the second row starts. My eyebrows release a cold, stinging sweat. I'm struggling to calculate the number of seconds each kid takes times the number of students left to go. My undershirt is soaked at the pits. The veins in my wrists bulge. Third row. Now we're at the "G"s. I'm the second "H" after Mike Hagan. He finishes his introduction and I panic as he sits down. My chest is so tight, I can barely inhale. I stand and immediately stare at the floor.

". . . . IIIIII'mm . . . . Jj-jjj-jjjjjjjOHN . . . . and . . . and . . . . . III . . . . jjjjj-jjjjjj-jjjjjjuST mmmooooved . . . . huh . . . . . huh . . . . huh-hhherre from . . . . Wwww-wuh-wuh-wwwwashington."

My teacher, Mr. Braithwaite, tries to play it cool. Eighteen years later, I stutter as I ask him about that day. I'm skeptical he'll remember anything. He remembers everything.

"So you stood up, lanky and gangly and no body fat, and the molecules in the room changed," he says. "Because everybody realized at the same moment . . . *Oh my God* . . . and there was a stillness, a hyper-vortex focus. I had so many sensations. There was my own guilt. How dare I put you in this position? Abject guilt, overwhelming empathy, a sense of protection that frankly continues to this day. I did not in any way want you to be hurt from this, and I sensed that you could. All the while, I was attempting to maintain my own composure, because as the kids in your class assessed what was happening, the vortex changed, and the attention suddenly went to me, like, 'You started this, what are you gonna do now?' I realized in that moment that the best possible thing I could do for you was to call upon my acting skills. And even though I just wanted to give you a hug or tell you to sit down, as the eyes went from you to me like a ping-pong, back and forth from the class, I realized that the greatest thing I could do was mask all of my anxiety for you, all of the guilt, and smile, and act like this was the most normal fucking thing that ever could happen on the planet. And, John, it took everything out of me to maintain, because while I'm putting on a happy face, I'm also going, 'Is this the right thing? Am I doing that? Am I doing right by him right now?'"

I went through eight of those introductions on my first day of ninth grade.

My new school was St. Joe's Prep, an all-male high school in North Philadelphia. Nearly all of my classmates walked into freshman year with five or ten or twenty kids they knew from grade school. Dozens had become fast friends over the summer during freshman football training camp. Many kids had older brothers who were upperclassmen. I didn't know a soul.

First day, fourth-period lunch. The cafeteria is massive, a sea of thirty tables filled with loud teenage guys. I grab a maroon tray from the stack and slide it along the metal ledge. I'm counting the kids in front of me again. I crane my neck to scan every item, trying to figure out which is the easiest to say. Now it's go time.

"Ffffffff . . . . . ffffffff . . . . . ."

The cafeteria lady's eyebrows scrunch together.

"Fffffff . . . uh . . . . . fffrrrrr . . . . . ."

I can't get to the "i." She throws me The Look.

Now the line behind me is longer.

"Ffffffff . . . ffffuh . . . ."

The kid next to me is laughing. Someone behind him shouts, *"What the fuck?"*

"Ffffff . . . . ffffRIES PLEASE."

She reaches across the sneeze guard and hands me the paper container with a pity smile. I stare at the floor and slide my tray along the ledge. I keep looking down as I wait in line to pay. Everyone else seems happy to be here. Some guys are walking around with pens resting on their ears and their shirts untucked. The woman behind the register hands me my change. I rest my tray on the condiment station and look out at the tables.

Where the hell do I sit?

7

Joe

Hi, John," Joe says. "Let's go back and talk."

I follow him down a long corridor and he opens the door to a windowless room with child-size furniture and toys. He sits down in one tiny seat and I hesitate to do the same. The embarrassment of having to return to therapy is only amplified by this room filled with colorful balls and Dr. Seuss books. Joe clicks his pen twice and scribbles on a fresh sheet of yellow legal pad paper.

"So, why do you want to come to therapy?"

". . . IIIII . . . . . . d-ddon't . . . . rrreally . . . . mmmmm-muh-my . . . . . mmmmom wants me to."

"All right, well then I guess we better bring her in here."

He leaves and returns a few minutes later with my mom. She looks confused.

"So, why do you want John to come to therapy?"

My mom looks over at me for an answer. Joe bounces a little yellow basketball against the table.

"Well, it's not that I want him to . . . it's . . . that we both think it's a good idea—John and I."

"John says he doesn't really want to be here. He says he's coming to please you."

My mom turns to me. She looks hurt.

"Is this true?" she asks.

I don't respond. The room is silent except for Joe's bouncing ball.

"Mr. Donaher, I was simply under the impression that this was what he wanted," she says. "We're all just trying to make things a little easier for him."

"Thank you, Mrs. Hendrickson. I'd like to talk to John now." She turns to leave. I feel horrible.

"Okay," Joe says. "Why are you here?"

MY SECONDARY BEHAVIORS had gotten out of control. I was now jerking my head toward my left shoulder every time I entered a block. Sometimes this would turn into a full up-and-under motion. It could happen over and over again, multiple times per sentence.

I'd made a few friends during freshman year but I sensed that they'd feel embarrassed when I'd blow up a sentence. I couldn't participate in jokes or quip like everyone else standing in a circle at our lockers. I felt guilty calling my friend Brendan's house—I knew I'd lose it on the "h" in "hello" if his brother or sister or dad answered. I was walking around with the sinking feeling that my classmates were pitying me—that I was the school charity case.

I showed up to freshman basketball tryouts alongside ninety other guys competing for about a dozen spots. I had played on competitive baseball teams and was called up to the eighth-grade basketball team as a seventh grader, but that was the past; none of it mattered now. I quickly learned that it's exponentially harder to make a team at a large all-boys high school. I was cut in the first round. In January I went out for the crew team. Tryouts consisted of two hours of intense workouts every day after school: push-ups and crunches and wall-sits and long runs through North Philadelphia in the dead of winter. Some days we'd run to the Philadelphia Museum of Art and race up and down the steps like Rocky. On Saturday mornings we'd show up early at school for timed sprints on the rowing machines in the basement. After making it through the first couple of rounds, I was once again cut. The coach offered me the inglorious position of manager. I took it. Every day I rode the bus to practice alongside everyone else, but the real athletes would eventually climb into the boats and row the Schuylkill River, while the other managers and I wandered around the boathouse, waiting for them to come back.

My skin was oily and pockmarked. My GPA was average. Had it not been for my stutter, I would have disappeared into the morass of my class, just another guy with brown hair shuffling through the halls. But I stood out, and not for an ideal reason. During sophomore year, some of my friendships faded and I was too afraid to ask myself why. I bounced around the outer rings of other friend groups without ever knowing if I'd get the call to come along that weekend. My parents would try to coax me into joining them for dinner at Bertucci's or some other suburban chain restaurant, but I would always say no. I couldn't bear the thought of facing a waiter after another long week at school. I spent a lot of Fridays renting DVDs from Blockbuster and eating a cheesesteak that my mom had ordered for me so I wouldn't have to deal with the counter guys at Paisano's. Soon I was avoiding even talking to my parents. I spent hours in my room reading and trudging through homework. My music taste started to get a little sadder: Radiohead, Elliott Smith. In some ways, I was a perfectly normal teenager, the insecure guy who reads *Catcher in the Rye* and thinks it's the Rosetta Stone. But instead of taking Holden Caulfield's wisdom at face value—that everyone *else* is a phony—I felt like the fraud.

There was one place where I glimpsed a better version of myself: AOL Instant Messenger. AIM was its own little ecosystem. The cafeteria hierarchy vanished. I could land jokes on AIM. I couldn't fathom trying to call a girl anymore, but typing something mildly clever into a chat box was doable. Sure, AIM had some cringey and performative elements to it. (How many Northeast high schoolers posted the lyrics to Dave Matthews Band's "Two Step" as their away message?) But the point of AIM was to have *conversations*. We had a family computer in a little corner room off our kitchen. I'd pull up the chair and type away—three, four, or five chats at once—sometimes until one or two in the morning. Of course, you were perpetually at risk of becoming the person who was *always* on AIM, which wasn't great either. But just communicating with other people every night helped. It was soothing. AIM was my chance to prove that I wasn't painfully awkward *all* the time. In this 2D, nonverbal world, I could even pass for normal. Then I'd wake up and go back to school.

"OKAY," JOE SAYS. "Why are you here?"

". . . . . . Be . . . . . . cause I can't . . . . rrr-really . . . . . talk."

"You can't talk, or you don't want to talk?"

". . . Um . . . . both."

"Do you talk on the phone much?"

". . . No."

"Do you participate in class often?"

"Oooo-cc-cuh-casionally."

"Do you find ways to avoid answering questions?"

"Yes."

"Do you eat out often?"

"No."

"Are you comfortable introducing yourself to new people?"

". . . . No."

This is five minutes into our first session. He's already unlike any speech therapist I've ever met. He's a big guy; my knuckles go white when he shakes my hand. He asks me about my favorite movies and TV shows and we riff about the Sixers and the Phillies. He starts juggling, telling me how before he went back to school he was an entertainer in Atlantic City. As the minutes tick by, I'm able to answer some of his questions without immediately looking down. At about the fifty-minute mark he tosses his legal pad on the table and sits back in his chair. Then he looks me dead in the eye.

"Well, John, you have a severe stutter."

He doesn't say it to be mean, but hearing it from someone else is a gut punch. I've been bullied and made fun of hundreds of times, but no adult has ever said that sentence that way. I don't know how to respond. He's not judging me. He's just stating a fact, like "The sky is blue" or "You have brown eyes." Still, it's disorienting. I'm fifteen years old. I've been to therapists and doctors and that strange hypnotist, and all of them went to great lengths to avoid even saying the word "stutter." It was always just my *problem,* my *issue,* my *impediment.* Joe clearly isn't worried about coddling me. He says it because it's true. He doesn't promise fluency, he just says, "I can help you stutter better."

We sit for a moment, then stand and walk back to the waiting room. My mom looks up from her magazine with a wounded smile.

"Okay, see you next week?" Joe says. It's a question, but he's not really asking. Before I answer he's already walking over toward his next patient, a boy much younger than I am.

The elevator dings. My mom and I are quiet. I can tell she wants to ask how it went but I sense she's also too afraid to say anything. We climb into the car and she pulls down the driver's-side visor to grab the parking garage ticket. I turn on the radio to break the silence.

"It was fffff-fine," I say. "He's cool."

My Wednesday ritual returns. Now I'm hurrying out of high school, hoping no one sees me getting into a car with my mom. Joe works out of Children's Hospital of Philadelphia. Thankfully we never open the kids' books. We don't even practice reading out loud.

A lot of Wednesdays we just sit there and talk about how much stuttering sucks, how this whole thing is a huge pain in the ass. I had never given myself permission to articulate that fact. It was always this thing you're not supposed to discuss, this silent burden, this embarrassment. My parents tried not to bring it up. I don't blame them. What were they supposed to say? *So, John, did you struggle again today?* Joe doesn't hide. It's freeing.

He shows me how my body language projects fear when I stutter—how my shoulders sink, how my chest turns concave. He explains that when I broadcast discomfort, people will respond with discomfort. My first project with Joe is to try to rebuild eye contact. This is extremely hard. I've spent more than a decade dreading the *moment* of stuttering, fearing The Look. I've cowered away from something as simple as ordering a red Gatorade from the school snack bar. The cashier is a nice woman, but that doesn't matter. Here's what usually happens: I wait until no one else is in line, then hustle over there. I imme-

diately enter an interminable block on the "r" sound in "red."
She turns and starts walking back toward the refrigerator. She
opens the glass door and moves her finger across the various
beverages, looking at me for a "yes" or "no" nod. It's like we're
playing Battleship, trying to hit the target. Now I'm pointing as
well, trying to help her, but still blocking on that "r." I'm almost
out of breath. She finally touches it and I hurriedly nod. She
rings me up and gives me my change with a pity smile.

I describe the saga to Joe and he immediately challenges me.

"Okay, so you're gonna go back tomorrow and not point," he
says. "Don't use your hands at all. You have to say it."

I feel like an idiot that this is even something I need to practice. Why is it so hard? Why does my whole body try to move
when I speak?

I reluctantly agree.

Okay, back at the snack bar:

". . . . . Rrrr . . . . . rrrruhhh . . . . rrrrr . . . ."

The cashier walks to the refrigerator.

". . . . Rrrrrrrr . . . . rrr . . ."

I'm blinking fast. My neck is throbbing. My lower back is wet
with sweat. Still no sound. Now too much time has elapsed. I
sense my arm rise. I half-heartedly point as my head jerks. She
grabs the bottle and rings me up.

I don't speak again for hours.

BY THIS POINT in high school, a lot of guys had girlfriends.
Some were already bragging about pregnancy scares. I felt
behind in everything. I worked a summer job at Genuardi's,
the local supermarket, bagging groceries and corralling shopping carts, barely speaking to the customers. My parents helped
me buy a used 1993 Chevy Cavalier coupe for two thousand

dollars. It had hand-crank windows and the steering wheel would shake if I pushed it above sixty-five. I mostly just drove it back and forth to school, though some days on my way home I would turn off just before crossing the Girard Avenue Bridge.

If you followed the curved road all the way, you'd eventually hit Kelly Drive and the Schuylkill River. But if you stopped midway down and pulled off on the shoulder, you might spot a long flight of old stone stairs just beyond the guardrail. As you descended the steps you'd dodge empty Smirnoff bottles and squished Newports; sometimes you'd see a torn condom wrapper or a needle. Once at the bottom you'd walk across a little meadow and climb a different set of steps that ran along the edge of the woods. This side had more trash: crushed twenty-four-ounce cans of Labatt Blue, broken forties of Olde English and Steel Reserve, ripped McDonald's bags. At the top of the stairs were multiple divergent paths through the trees. If you followed the long, winding trail to the left it led to a clearing overlooking the river.

Next time you're riding the Amtrak north to New York City, just after the Philadelphia Zoo, take a look out the right-side window as you cross the bridge and you'll see it: an open-faced rock formation covered in graffiti. You may notice some high school kids lounging on the rock's edge. This is where I first smoked weed.

Stoners were more approachable than the other guys at school. They spoke softer and their hair was shaggier. But above all they just seemed nicer and less judgmental. They were the polar opposite of all the football players who careened through the hallways like snowplows. If you were looking to get high on a given day after school, you could just show up at the rock, and a few people would be there. Someone would pass you a blunt or a bowl. You'd be greeted with a smile even if you weren't part of the group. It wasn't really a group. People would come and go.

I wouldn't head to the spot every day, but when I did go, I felt at peace. In time I started stealthily buying dime bags in the senior parking lot to smoke by myself at night. I'd hide the little baggie in a pocket of my backpack, then panic on the drive home, looking in my rearview mirror, thinking every set of headlights was a cop. I'd go upstairs and lock the baggie in the second drawer of the file cabinet under my desk. I'd hide the key under the round plastic display case holding my Cal Ripken autographed baseball near the top of my bookshelf. At night, after everyone went to sleep, I'd retrieve the little nuggets, then roll a dried bud between my fingers, studying it over and over. I'd crack the window and spark a bowl and exhale smoke out into the suburban night. My lungs would feel full and fiery. I loved smoking weed. It was quiet. Rhythmic. Meditative. I'd eventually climb in bed and listen to music and stare at the slanted ceiling, drifting off to sleep, thinking about some mythical future morning when I'd wake up and magically stop stuttering. But weed didn't solve my problems. That was beer's job.

8

Liquid Courage

Occasionally I'd swipe green bottles of Rolling Rock from the back of the kitchen fridge, but I truly came to know beer as the foamy, trickling stream filling a Solo cup in the middle of a dark field. All throughout high school, there was a standing kegger each weekend in a dodgy section of Fairmount Park. Seniors would buy kegs of Natty Light from a North Philly distributor with a lax (or nonexistent) ID policy, then charge five bucks for an endlessly refillable cup to whoever showed up. Somewhere between fifty and a hundred high schoolers would be there on Saturday nights, milling around in circles, even in the middle of winter.

It's hard to write about my relationship with beer. Neither of my parents ever drank more than a glass of wine with dinner, but one of my grandmothers was an alcoholic. I've always had an extremely high tolerance. As a teenager, beer became a crutch. It doesn't get me drunk, it just puts me at ease. I sometimes think of sipping a beer like putting on an old sweatshirt.

My stutter greatly diminishes when I drink. This isn't surprising or revelatory; alcohol is a depressant with documented effects on the brain, and stuttering is a neurological disorder. Beer started bringing me closer to the person I was on AIM—the guy who could chime into group conversations, someone who could say "Yes, and . . ." during a joke and actually make people laugh. It really does have a way of numbing some problems. None of this is ideal, but it's true.

I remember the therapy session during junior year when I told Joe how my stutter quieted down when I drank. I said it to him like I was revealing a secret. He gave me a serious look.

"That's fine for now," he said. "But you have to watch it."

JIM McKAY KNEW WHERE his dad kept the Jim Beam. He learned how to sneak a pour of bourbon and top the bottle off with water so his parents couldn't tell anything was missing. This was sophomore year of high school; he'd mix it with Coca-Cola and head to a party like any other fifteen-year-old in his Chicago suburb.

Jim had a stutter that humiliated him and had evolved into a major source of anxiety. Drinking helped him relax, though once he started he didn't know how to stop. He'd frequently drink to the point of blacking out, and the next morning his anxiety could be even more intense than it was before his first sip. Some mornings he'd lie in bed hungover, worrying about what he might have said or done the previous night. It was a vicious cycle: The more self-conscious he felt, the more he stuttered. This increased his overall anxiety, which led him to drink more. His behavior was unpredictable. Sometimes he'd drink in the mornings before first period. "By the time I was eighteen, I'm sure I met diagnostic criteria for alcohol dependence," he later told me.

Jim is now in his mid-sixties, with curly gray hair and a salt-and-pepper beard. He lives outside Philadelphia and works in the psychiatry department at the University of Pennsylvania medical school, where he specializes in addiction and substance abuse. Though I wouldn't know it until years later when he wrote me a letter, I used to pass through Jim's neighborhood on my way home from cold nights standing around the field drinking endless cups of beer to feel better about myself.

Jim's been stuttering for more than half a century. Shortly after his younger sister was born, he told his mother that he didn't think he could talk anymore. She took him to see the family pediatrician, who prescribed a "special pill" to fix his problem. It didn't work; he later learned it was a placebo. His stutter kept getting worse as he progressed through childhood. He dreaded introductions—he could usually force out "Jim" but would block hard on "McKay." During class presentations, he'd stand at the front of the room sweating, his hands shaking. His parents later took him to a speech clinic at Northwestern University, but therapy didn't really work either.

As a teenager, a football injury ended his athletic career. He began retreating further into himself. Soon he was avoiding speaking in many public situations. He became a straight-D student and was regularly blacking out in the evenings as he trudged through school. Then his parents' marriage started falling apart. Like many midwestern families, the McKays could keep up appearances during the day, but sometimes Jim would wake up in the middle of the night to the sound of his parents arguing in their bedroom.

"I think there were, like, money issues and stuff, and one of the things I remember them arguing about was whether I should still be in speech therapy," Jim told me. "I remember my father saying, 'Well, you know, it's important that he do that.' It's the only time I've ever heard my father even mention anything about my speech. Clearly it was on his mind, but he would not talk about it with me."

Jim's parents divorced when he was sixteen. He was playing in bands and as a senior didn't bother to apply to college, partially because he dreaded the thought of speaking in front of new people. "I think stutterers tend to feel so acutely aware of people listening, and it's hard to get out from under that," Jim said. "Drinking and taking drugs were ways of trying to feel, you know, less uncomfortable."

While alcohol remained his drug of choice, he eventually moved on to stimulants and psychedelics. When he was high, Jim felt like he could say anything to anybody. He was particularly fond of MDA, a precursor to MDMA. He loved the way the drug obliterated his self-consciousness and, even better, his feelings of shame. One night, after taking multiple doses of MDA at a party, he returned home at four in the morning. He walked around back and climbed in the above-ground pool. It was the middle of winter. Jim's stepfather found him the next morning, just moving around in the water, completely out of his mind. It's a miracle he didn't develop hypothermia or drown. Near a breaking point in his early twenties, he slowly began putting the rest of his life together. He started attending Alcoholics Anonymous meetings in and around Chicago. He's now been sober for decades.

"When I finally went to AA, it was a room full of people saying, 'Yeah, well, you think you're screwed up? Here's what I did.' There was such a sense of being with other people who were like me, at least in that way. That was so comforting. And I've oftentimes thought, Why don't I go to, like, a Stutterers Anonymous? Like, why am I so alone with that? What is it about stuttering that makes you bear the burden yourself? There seems to be something that we experience that is so shameful. And you can't talk about it, even though it's obvious."

Jim completed an undergraduate psychology degree at Loyola University in Chicago, then pursued a master's, and eventually a Ph.D., at Harvard. When the day arrived to defend his master's thesis, he stuttered horribly in front of the panel of instructors. He left the room, shaking with embarrassment, then stepped onto an elevator filled with his fellow grad students, some of whom had just watched him struggle through every minute of his oral presentation. A developmental psychology professor turned to him and made a disparaging remark about his "nervousness." Jim was mortified. Later that day, he walked to the professor's office to confront him.

"I said, 'I have a stutter, and it's really, really hard for me to get in front of groups of people—and it was humiliating, what you said.'" The professor scoffed at him. "He said, 'You clearly have a huge problem here if you can't take any sort of constructive criticism.'" Jim was stunned. "He basically said, 'I would never want to work with you.'"

Jim and I first spoke at length in October 2020, then again one evening after Thanksgiving. He has a warm, caramel voice, like a young Willie Nelson. He told me he had only occasionally talked about his stutter, and never in much depth before our first conversation. In the intervening weeks, he had started to open up a bit more to his adult daughters about his lifelong struggle.

"I felt more comfortable talking with them about my substance abuse history than I did about my speech," Jim told me. "All the men on my mom's and my dad's sides of the family have all had hideous alcohol problems, so I just really felt they needed to know, in terms of their own drinking, and be aware of some vulnerabilities that they might have there," he said. "But the speech stuff—when I told them I was going to be talking with you again—my younger daughter said, 'Who's that? You didn't tell me about that.' So, I do feel like there's still in me some degree of embarrassment, or hesitation to talk with them about it. Even as I'm a little more open, it just is a reminder of how closed-off I had been. They're really interested—that's the other thing. It's just another thing about Dad that they want to know. It's not some sort of horrible thing that they're uncomfortable with."

On a recent trip home to see my parents, I met Jim for breakfast. We sat down at a cafe in the shopping center where I used to bag groceries—back when I was too afraid to speak to the customers. I brought up how hard it can be to disclose the fact that you stutter, at any age, even to those who are close to you. Jim told me how frustrated he was feeling lately that he sometimes struggles to speak fluently around his wife, someone he's known and loved for more than thirty years. I told him how I hadn't stopped thinking about his "Stutterers Anonymous" quote ever since he said it. Why is it that so many of us keep this part of our lives so hidden? Jim compared and contrasted it with addiction: People in recovery are proud to be sober, and many want to help others in a group setting. But there's one key difference.

"You may stop drinking," Jim said, "whereas you'll never stop stuttering."

9

Black Waves

By the winter of junior year, I had been working with Joe for more than twelve months, but I was still avoiding everyday situations. I was looking down more than I was looking up. I had started second-guessing almost everything I had to say. I was substituting words so often that my sentences barely made sense: *Did yy-you . . . . . . sss-ee . . . . the big hit . . . . . um . . . . Phillies . . . win the game?*

I bought a Pearl drum set and would release some of my stress on it down in the basement. Occasionally I'd invite two friends over to jam on their black-and-white Squier Stratocasters. (Nobody ever wants to play bass.) We'd run through hiccupy renditions of Weezer's "Island in the Sun," then spend hours brainstorming band names, even though we would never play a gig and therefore never need a name. When the weekend rolled around, I'd show up at the field and refill my red cup of Natty Light, trying to find the guts to talk to people. Late at night, after I got home, a neighborhood friend would squeeze through the gap in the fence and wait for me on my front porch. I'd sneak a few beers from the fridge and he and I would drink and smoke weed and turn into high school philosophers.

But junior year was when I really started shutting down.

I used lame excuses like "a lot of homework" to skip many of my sessions with Joe. He was pushing me to talk about both my stutter and speech therapy in general with my family, but I couldn't fathom bringing it up. I still felt guilty stuttering around my parents—I was almost seventeen and had been seeing therapists for over a decade, and for what? I was ashamed at my lack of progress. I assumed they must be, too.

My mom would ask me about my day and I'd respond with one-word answers. I'd stare down at my plate, carry it to the kitchen, then retreat to the TV room or my bedroom. I'd space out doing homework, waste hours until it was time to go to bed, then lie awake, listening to CDs, struggling to sleep. I stalled until the last possible minute to get up each morning. I didn't feel sorry for myself; I felt apathetic.

Days and weeks and months merged together. I noticed that I was taking stairs slower. My hair was messier and I wouldn't always shower. I followed the same track almost every day: bed, car, school, car, dinner, TV room, bedroom, bed. After particularly hard days at school, and strained nights at home, the last thing I wanted was to talk about what was going on, even with people on AIM. I started spending a lot of time upstairs, obsessing over bad blocks from hours before, digging my fingers into the right side of a corduroy chair. I worried that I had become a burden to my friends and began to question what they were getting out of my presence. One night that winter, I couldn't sleep, and, after staring at the ceiling above my bed for a while, I whispered a short sentence: *Maybe I'm depressed.* It was out of my mouth before I could shove it back in. It terrified me. I never said this sentence to my parents. I never had the courage to say it to Joe. I never wrote it publicly until writing this paragraph. I see it up there on the page and I'm still unmoored when I read it. But depression doesn't care if you acknowledge its existence. It's quiet. It's patient.

I'm forever grateful that the depression I've known hasn't taken more from me. I've frequently thought about being dead, but I've never made a plan to get there. Even in the depths of my depression, during high school, I could still get out of bed. Again: lucky. Everyone who comes to know depression meets a different version of it. I could still do some things very well. I'd read books on a deep level and I received A's on nearly every English assignment. I wrote little stories and poems and songs even though I could only sort of play the drums and couldn't read music. I'd see my favorite bands at the Electric Factory and the TLA and I became a regular, nonverbal presence at a coffeehouse called the Point. I still cracked up at *The Simpsons*. But then waves of black would roll in. Sometimes I could push through them, and sometimes they knocked me over. I didn't know when, if ever, I'd feel the way I used to feel before depression entered my life. I've learned to manage it, but I still don't know if I'll ever fully return to that predepression point. But again: *lucky*. I'll never *not* feel lucky. I'm lucky to be able to sit here and write the sentence that scares me.

MUKESH ADHIKARI also considers himself lucky. He grew up mainly in Kathmandu, Nepal, the middle of three siblings. He barely spoke until he was four years old, then began to stutter between the ages of five and six. His parents took him to a doctor, who assured them that their son's problem would fade away as he got older. Adhikari's uncle and cousins also had stutters, but theirs were mild. Despite his disfluency, Adhikari excelled academically. He was at or near the top of his class through elementary and middle school and eventually learned three languages: Nepali, Hindi, and English. But his stutter never improved as he aged. Once he became a teenager, his disfluency started taking over his life. He was frequently lodged in endless blocks, holding his mouth open for seconds at a time, waiting for missing sounds to appear. He was frustrated by his inability to say even basic things. Sometimes his stutter made him feel like he was literally choking.

As a high schooler, Adhikari researched the chemical makeup of the brain, looking for answers to his problem. He learned that speech production occurs in the Broca's area, in the frontal lobe, and for a short while he took to ramming his head against a wall. Something told him that pummeling his brain might stimulate activity in the cerebral cortex and, perhaps, rewire the neural pathways that caused his broken speech. It didn't work.

He was perpetually embarrassed, and, by sophomore year, he was no longer the best student in his class. He refused to talk about his daily struggles with his parents or siblings or anyone else. Soon the pain became unbearable. Many days Adhikari would come home from school, shut the door to his bedroom, and sob. By sixteen, the weight of stuttering had gotten too heavy. He was considering ways to kill himself.

One day Adhikari locked himself in his bedroom. He sat down. He had reached his breaking point, no longer feeling fit to interact with the outside world. He sat quietly, waiting. And then something pushed him to meditate. His parents had raised their children to embrace spirituality—they would regularly practice meditation at a nearby temple. Adhikari worked to steady his breathing, to center himself, to move his mind away from his obsessive thoughts about stuttering. After nearly four hours in that locked room, he glimpsed a subtle sense of calm and, for the first time in a while, optimism. He kept meditating through high school, and, eventually, his suicidal thoughts receded.

He went on to college and worked for six years in the Ministry of Health and Population of Nepal. When he was twenty-six, he fell in love, and for the first time opened up to someone about what life is like as a person who stutters. The two married and later moved to Connecticut, where he pursued a master's in health policy at Yale. He was living in New Haven when we first spoke. On the night Adhikari told me about coming to the brink, I asked him how he felt about me including his story in this book. I told him that, if necessary, I could conceal his identity—using just his initials, or a pseudonym.

"You can use my first name," he said flatly.

Near the end of our conversation, he changed his mind.

"If you want to place my full name—first name and last name—you can do that," Adhikari said. He had never told his parents how close he came to committing suicide, but he no longer wanted to hide it. He talked about how stuttering had made him a stronger listener and how grateful he is for that part of his life.

"A lot of people out there struggle," he said. "People have to think that there is some sort of silver lining."

GERALD MAGUIRE'S older brother, Charles, didn't see any other option. The two were companion stutterers in a family of seven. They grew up on the edge of the Sierra Nevada mountains in Paradise, California, about ninety miles north of Sacramento. In the fall of 2018, their town made national headlines when it was nearly wiped off the map by an apocalyptic wildfire. But a decade and a half before that, Charles, whose severe disfluency was compounded by severe depression, took his own life.

"He had such pride as the oldest brother, and to see him suffer like he did was a lot," Maguire told me. "Even thinking about it now—it's hard. But there's a lot of Charleses out there."

Maguire speaks in quick bursts and frames most of his statements in the form of questions. He has a California tan and a face that periodically relaxes into a wide grin. He'll pepper your first name into the middle of a sentence and cap his thoughts with a quick "Right?" or "Does that make sense?" to make sure you and he are still connected.

Maguire is a professor of psychiatry at California University of Science and Medicine. He was a consultant for the most recently revised version of the *Diagnostic and Statistical Manual of Mental Disorders,* which attempted to rebrand stuttering as "childhood-onset fluency disorder." (Nevertheless, most people still call it stuttering.) Maguire has spent decades researching pharmaceutical solutions to treat various neurological disorders, stuttering in particular. Until he laid it out for me, I had never considered the physical similarities that stuttering shares with ADHD and Tourette syndrome—the rapid blinking, the jaw clenching, the various motor tics. Then he told me about the commonalities between stuttering and OCD.

"There are interrelationships in the subcortical regions of the brain on this thalamocortical loop that is all out of whack in OCD—and similar in stuttering," Maguire said. (I don't understand at least two of those words, but let's keep going.)

When he was a kid, every year on New Year's Eve he'd head down to the creek near his house and walk in an identical loop ten times in a row. He convinced himself that if he did this with enough focus, he'd stop stuttering. It didn't work, but each new year would come and he'd make his pilgrimage to the water, moving in circles, repeating his repetitions.

Many stutterers obsess about challenging words coming down the line in a sentence. Some stutterers plan multiple words or phrases ahead to avoid tripping over just one small sound. "This is very similar to obsessive-compulsive thought-process behavior," Maguire told me. "I think we're at the point with stuttering where we were thirty years ago with obsessive-compulsive disorder. You grew up with the term 'OCD,' but people in the seventies had never heard of it."

While listening to him speak, I started going over my own rituals, my stuttering tics, all the OCD tendencies in my life. Sometimes I get trapped in a cycle of writing sentences that end with three short clauses, like this one, right here.

A little later on in our conversation, I told him something I haven't shared with many people. "I've had . . . . . a . . . lifelong anxiety that . . . . my parents were . . . . gonna die in a car crash."

"That's an obsessive thought!" he said. Then he repeated it.

"I have . . . one hundred of those things," I confessed. "I have anxiety about, like, getting a prostate exam. I have a whole bunch of stuff like that, um, to the point that, in the past decade of my life . . ."

"There you go!" he said. "So that's what—" He stopped himself, clicking into psychiatrist mode. "Please go on."

"There's a Radiohead song called 'Everything in Its Right Place'—and that's how I feel," I said. "Like if there's a pile of magazines on the coffee table . . . . I need the . . . . magazines to be . . . . I need everything in its right place."

"I see your need to have control of your environment," he said. "So hey, there you go: *Realization!* And I'm just gonna put this out there: you're living it, John. That's probably why you reached out to me, right?"

It was jarring to acknowledge the possibility of another disorder hanging around my brain besides a stutter. I felt like I was going the wrong way down a moving sidewalk at the airport. I started thinking back through childhood. Was I manically tossing the pen up and down while on the phone, or was I watching it rise and fall exactly three times in my hand? Why did I wiggle the same three toes on the same foot every time I entered an awful block? I remembered how in the first grade I used to repeat sentences in a soft whisper after finally forcing them out. When my mom would help me put on my socks in preschool I needed the stitches to line up perfectly across my toes or I'd feel unsettled all day.

I started humming the Radiohead song I had mentioned to Maguire. It's the opening track on *Kid A:*

> *Everything*
> *Everything*
> *Everything*
> *Everything*
> *In its right place*
> *In its right place*
> *In its right place*
> *In its right place*

I've listened to this song hundreds of times, but I've never noticed the OCD-like construction of the lyrics until typing them out just now. And what is it that made me want to play drums instead of any other instrument in the first place? Why did I love spending hours in a basement repeating rhythmic patterns? I can still see myself down there, under the exposed pipes, obsessing over simple 4/4 beats, all four limbs moving at once. Was this my escape from stuttering or a manifestation of my need for control?

Maguire's medical school professors told him not to pursue psychiatry. His voice changed as he shared this memory with me. He said he was told to consider radiology, or some other job where he could "sit in a basement and not talk to people." In many areas of medicine, you're required to pass a timed oral exam before you can become a doctor. (Among Maguire's many in-the-works projects is the formation of a legal defense fund for medical students who believe they face discrimination based on the structure of the certification system.)

He's been profiled in newspapers and magazines and he's served as the chairman of the National Stuttering Association, yet many members of the stuttering community take issue with his approach to the disorder. For years, under the guidance of his own physician, Maguire has been taking prescription medication that is not specifically approved for stuttering, but is typically used to help other neurological conditions. Still, whenever you hear someone talk about a potential "magic pill" to fix stuttering once and for all, Maguire's name will come up. This is where he turns some folks off. The first question you typically hear is *Why should stutterers take drugs to make their brains conform to the expectations of an ableist society?*

"Acceptance in any condition is always the first step for therapy," Maguire counters. "In order to get therapy for cancer, you have to accept it to get the treatment. They're not mutually exclusive. It doesn't have to be an either/or. And why should stuttering be any different than depression or hypertension?"

Those who support a chemical-based approach to treating stuttering, like Maguire, spend a lot of time thinking about neurotransmitters and how we might be able to manipulate them. Neurotransmitters are molecules that aid in communication among neurons in the brain—as well as between neurons and various muscles in the body. One of the most well-known neurotransmitters is dopamine. We often hear people talk about "dopamine hits," or the rush of satisfaction to the brain that can sometimes feel like pleasure is washing over your whole body. We can get a dopamine release from something as simple as taking a run in the park on a sunny day. Some people get dopamine boosts from listening to music or from posting a photo to Instagram and watching the likes roll in. Maguire and other researchers have hypothesized that stutterers have an imbalance of the activity of dopamine in their brains, creating problems along neural pathways, leading to broken speech. They believe that true fluency may be attained by *blocking* the release of dopamine. You can imagine the downsides: Why would we want less of a bodily chemical that makes us feel good?

Maguire has also given a lot of consideration to GABA, gamma-aminobutyric acid. (I can barely say that one out loud.) GABA is another neurotransmitter, but rather than support communication, GABA blocks impulses between neurons in the brain: it's an inhibitor in this sense. When a person "releases their inhibitions," they're less self-conscious about both what they're saying and how they're saying it. Alcohol aids this process, for better or worse. As I discovered as a fifteen-year-old, drinking a beer—or two, or three—will help my muscles relax. And, as I divulged to Joe, a slight beer buzz helps me worry a little less about my stutter, and it can even help me speak more fluently. This isn't a placebo effect; it's real brain chemistry. And not long after that first sip reaches your brain, GABA kicks in. It's a slippery slope.

"It's not going to be simple—one neurotransmitter, one disorder. There's nothing like that," Maguire said. "Depression isn't that way. Obsessive-compulsive disorder isn't that way. Yeah, I can say, 'Stuttering is a dopamine-mediator disorder,' but that's not the entire story. There is an interplay of GABA, dopamine, serotonin, others—they all have different neurotransmitter actions, but they all relate."

Maguire and other researchers may have finally found an anti-stuttering drug in the form of a dopamine blocker called Ecopipam. It's currently in clinical trials, and Maguire is cautiously optimistic about the results. However, in a turn of dark irony, one of Ecopipam's most serious potential side effects is depression—the mental disorder that, along with stuttering, led Maguire's older brother to take his own life. That these two neurological problems are bound up in each other is not lost on him.

Because of the media attention that has accompanied his research over the past two decades, Maguire regularly receives emails from stutterers all over the world. Some people ask him for access to the drugs he's working on, side effects be damned. Many of them write to him about the debilitating anxiety that stuttering has brought into their life. Some stutterers talk to Maguire about wanting to kill themselves. He reads all the messages and tries to respond to each one, but every time a new article comes out with his name in it, another flood of mail arrives.

"It's not an obligation," he said. "It's a calling. Isn't that different?"

If Ecopipam eventually receives FDA approval, I honestly don't know if I'll take it. Some days I'd jump at the chance to never, ever talk this way again. But the thought of swallowing a pill to neutralize part of my DNA feels a bit like a cop-out. I hate the fact that stuttering introduced depression into my life as a teenager, but I'm grateful for the empathy and understanding it's given me since. No, I do not always like who I am when I stutter. But would I recognize myself if I didn't stutter?

10

Kairos

One day my grandparents put my dad on a one-way train from Illinois to Alabama. Though barely a teenager, he was to step off and begin preparing for the priesthood at an all-boys Catholic seminary. His older brother, Marty, was already there. At age twenty-one, six weeks before taking his vows, my dad walked away. My uncle had already dropped out. Many of their classmates would do the same. As kids, Matt and I never got a concrete answer as to what really happened. My dad said only that it was complicated, that his heart was no longer in it. It was always a strange nugget of family history: *Have you heard the one about Dad's other life?* Sometimes we'd joke about how he and my mom wouldn't have met—how my brother and I wouldn't exist—had my dad gone through with it, had he actually become a priest. Eventually I learned one of his reasons for quitting: my dad and several of his classmates had been sexually abused.

I first heard that part of the story around the time *The Boston Globe* published its massive investigation into pervasive sexual abuse and cover-ups in the Catholic Church. As the scandal began to seep out beyond Boston, there was renewed interest in some of my dad's writing from the early 1980s about his experience. He had been manipulated, forced to carry a secret, then made to feel ashamed. I felt sorry for my dad, but I was also deeply proud of him for writing about it.

After the shock wore off, I had some self-centered questions: Why did my parents still choose to raise a Catholic family? Why did they send Matt and me to Catholic schools?

In the fall of my senior year, my old history teacher, an ordained deacon, resigned because of allegations that he had kissed students earlier in his career. He walked out of school one afternoon in November and never came back. In 2011, Matt's former Latin teacher, a Jesuit priest, pleaded guilty to two counts of fourth-degree sexual offense after being credibly accused of fondling two students. He was forced to register as a sex offender. This priest had moved among several East Coast parishes—he worked at my high school in Philadelphia for five years before he taught at Matt's in Maryland.

In the two decades since the *Globe* reporters exposed these patterns in the Catholic Church—as depicted in the stellar movie *Spotlight*—thousands of other Catholics have come forward with stories of abuse. Several of the people I grew up with have abandoned Catholicism as adults, but far more have stayed loyal to the Church. These days, when I open Instagram, I scroll past photos of weddings and baptisms. I see old classmates posing on altars next to grinning priests in flowing vestments. The people in these photos always look genuinely happy. In many families, but especially in Catholic families, you don't question God or the Church, you just smile and show up and teach your kids to do the same. We've all got our problems; there are some things you just don't talk about. Plus: we're all sinners. That's why we go to church—to pray and repent. It's a system. It works.

Why do so many Catholic families move through life upholding the traditions of guilt, shame, and secrecy?

I wish I could say that I stopped caring about the Church after I graduated from high school, but doing so would ignore one of the most important experiences of my stuttering life, which took place at a Catholic-school event shrouded in secrecy.

It's difficult for me to write about this, because I'm still afraid to question how it happened. I never considered myself a Catholic-with-a-capital-C. Most families dutifully went to church every Sunday; we'd go only on Christmas and Easter, and not every year. I dragged my feet through the three sacraments you receive as a kid after you're baptized: Reconciliation, Communion, and Confirmation.

That first one still baffles me. What sins are you supposed to confess as a seven-year-old? I can see myself closing the door to the little room in the back of the sanctuary. I take a seat and the priest asks me what I'm there to talk about. I ponder the question for a few moments.

Well . . . Father . . . I kicked the basketball at recess today.

Why did you do that?

Because I'm a sinner.

Do you feel guilty?

Yes.

And what are you seeking?

God's forgiveness.

Tell God you're sorry. Ask him to absolve you of your sins.

Okay. I'm sorry, God. I am a bad person for kicking the basketball.

This is the kind of ritual that's ingrained in Catholic children well before they grasp the more important and nuanced concept of free will. Year after year, you're taught to feel guilty for both mundane and serious offenses alike. You're told it's an honor to drink Jesus's blood and eat his flesh, and you're constantly reminded that he died for our sins. *Your* sins. Jesus died so you can kick the basketball at recess, and now it's your job to feel guilty about it. I showed up. I smiled. I prayed. I followed this pattern because that's what was expected of me.

In eighth grade, when my classmates and I were preparing for Confirmation—the moment you fully accept God into your life—I told my mom I didn't want to go through with it, that I no longer believed any of it. She assured me that it was okay to just pay lip service. She approached the situation pragmatically: Confirmation was a necessary step if, in the future, I fell in love with a girl who wanted to have a Catholic wedding.

I felt nauseous at the image of me down on one knee, jerking my head and hyperventilating through a marriage proposal as a faceless woman looked on in horror. I tried not to think about having to stand up in a church full of people and stutter horribly through my wedding vows. I wondered if I could ever find a partner who wasn't embarrassed by my still-getting-worse problem.

I used to pray to God to help me talk better. I wouldn't say, "Please help me stop stuttering"; I'd say, "Please help me work on my speech." By that I mean I always took responsibility. I was never waiting for divine intervention, some unannounced invasion of the Holy Spirit, a warm and all-powerful glow running through me.

And then one day I felt exactly that.

KAIROS IS A GREEK WORD that means both "the right time" and "God's time"—at least that's what the school told us. I like Merriam-Webster's definition a little better: "A time when conditions are right for the accomplishment of a crucial action: the opportune and decisive moment."

Kairos is a four-day retreat that Jesuit prep schools offer every year for juniors and seniors. Jesuits, more than any other sect of Catholicism, preach the idea of *cura personalis,* or the development of the "whole person." Almost every Jesuit institution requires dozens of hours of community service in order to graduate. Aside from earning a diploma, the apex of a modern Jesuit high school education is experiencing Kairos. About fifty students go on the retreat at a given time. It's a voluntary activity, but hardly anyone opts out. After all, you get to miss three full days of school.

Almost everything about Kairos is kept secret, and as ridiculous as it sounds, I feel obligated to uphold those secrets. To be clear: nothing about Kairos is dark or medieval. There are no creepy basement rituals with robes and chants like you've seen in Hollywood depictions of Skull and Bones or other secret societies. One of the key influences on Kairos is transcendentalism. The typical retreat house is located in a secluded natural area, and you spend a fair amount of time walking in nature, reflecting on your life.

Kairos, at least as I came to experience it, isn't really about the Bible. It's a fairly casual few days, lacking many of the traditional stuffy components of church. There are numerous events that mark dramatic turns in the retreat, and, unfortunately, that stuff falls under the "secret" category. Here's what I feel comfortable divulging, if only because it's one of the few "open" secrets: retreat leaders deliver speeches about particular struggles in their lives.

It's tough to become a Kairos leader. Many former retreat attendees apply, but only a handful are selected. You spend weeks or months preparing a thirty-minute speech, driving toward a central message that you believe will help others in some way.

Up until this point, the fall of my senior year, I had been excused from giving most oral presentations on account of my stutter. I was embarrassed about this, but I was even more afraid to stand up and speak in front of my peers. Looking back on it now, I still can't believe I ever applied to be a Kairos leader. I'm sure I was quietly doubting that I'd actually get picked. When I got the call, I was overwhelmed, and terrified.

I wrote the first draft of my speech by hand in a green spiral notebook. It began:

9/9/05

There's not a day that goes by in which I don't feel embarrassed about the way that I talk. Stuttering is a large burden in my life, and I often find myself asking how things ~~could~~ might be different if I could speak fluently.

My handwriting is shaky and angular. I think I crossed out "could" and replaced it with "might" because the former betrays possibility and the latter has an undercurrent of doubt. However, even if I had woken up the next day without a stutter, my emotional baggage and insecurity were so deep-seated at that point that I wonder if anything would have really changed. But maybe I'm overanalyzing one sentence. Maybe I crossed out "could" because the same word appears a little later down the line and I was trying to avoid repetition.

I spent weeks sitting in my room tinkering with the speech. By that point in high school, I used what little money I saved to buy musical gear: new Remo drumheads, Vic Firth sticks of all weights and sizes, a set of bongos, a TASCAM four-track analog recorder, and, most important, a microphone. Night after night I'd go down to the basement and rehearse my speech into the mic, trying to desensitize my brain to the sound of my amplified voice. It always made me cringe: *Is that really what I sound like?* I'd take a seat on a wobbly wooden stool, plug in the mic, and read out loud to an invisible audience. Even among unfolded laundry, I couldn't speak fluently. I timed myself every day like a runner training for a marathon, trying to shave off minutes. I was always out of breath and sweating by the end. One day after school I read the speech aloud to my old religion teacher, Mr. Braithwaite, in his empty classroom. He cried.

Not long ago, I found the final typed version—ten pages—buried in a long gray envelope. I had separated all the sentences into three-to-five-word chunks with backslashes in blue ink. I had underlined the first vowel in each phrase, just like they used to appear in my old speech-therapy practice texts.

I was the final speaker on the first night of Kairos. The white paper rattled in my fingers as I walked to the lectern. I adjusted the mic toward my mouth. It was just after ten p.m., and everyone in the room was exhausted. At Joe's suggestion, I opened with a caveat:

Before I begin / I just wanna tell you / that I stutter / and that this might take / longer for me / than it has / for other people.

(No shit.)

The purpose of a disclosure like this is to ease the tension in the room—to acknowledge what everyone is thinking. In an ideal scenario, nodding to the presence of your stutter makes things *less* awkward for the audience. But I stuttered dreadfully through that simple disclosure. Here's what the introduction actually sounded like:

". . . . . B . . . . buh . . . .
. . . . . beeeef . . . . before I . . . .
b . . . . be, uh . . . . begin . . . . I . . . .
. . . . I just . . . ."

There were roughly fifty people in the room, including seven teachers serving as chaperones. It took me ten minutes to reach page two. As I gulped and blocked over each marked-up phrase, I could feel my lungs rapidly contracting. I was struggling to breathe. My legs trembled. I felt like I was suspended in a slow-motion free fall, like the animation in the opening credits of *Mad Men*. This was the most severe disfluency I'd experienced since the first day of freshman year. I felt every pinch of my lips, every buckle in my throat. My jaw was locked in a bear trap.

And then suddenly I was floating above myself, watching myself stutter. My neck was warm, but not the way it is when I'm anxious. This was a comforting warmth, like a hot water bottle on your upset stomach. When I looked up, everyone was patiently listening. The room was quiet except for the cracks and puffs and serrated breath coming through the mic. No one was laughing. Nobody was giving me The Look. I glanced over to one of the guys I sometimes played music with and saw him fighting tears.

I had first gone on Kairos as a participant about six months earlier, near the end of my junior year. One night that week I had been enveloped in the same softening warmth. It ran through my whole body. A phrase from one of the speeches I heard echoed in my mind all summer—I can still hear the person saying it right now. I gestured to it during my own speech.

On my Kairos / I learned / that every single person / in here / is carrying around / their own bag of hammers. / I learned that

/ yeah / I struggle / but so does everyone else / We all have at least / one major problem in our lives . . .

How do you carry a bag of hammers? It's heavy. It's awkward. Do hammers even come in a bag? Who cares. *Bag of hammers.*

When I reached the end of my speech I forced out a quiet "thank you" and started walking back to my seat. The room filled with applause. It was part eruption, part exhale. I saw many people wiping their eyes. I was numb. The speech had taken me over an hour to read. It felt like five hours. The applause continued and I nervously looked down at the floor. I sensed the warm pulsating feeling again: a presence. I didn't hear a booming voice or glimpse a bright light. It was just warm. I received a telepathic message to let go. *Enough. Let go.*

I formed a bond with some of the guys on that Kairos that continued all year, and it held firm for many years thereafter. But none of us ever talked about the speech I gave, or any of the other speeches. We agreed to keep everything a secret, and I kept my end of the bargain until writing about it here. I'll carry many other Kairos secrets for the rest of my life.

When I look back on my Catholic education, which began as a three-year-old in nursery school and ended as a shaving high school senior, there are so many aspects of it that I loathe, and judge, and resent. I still fundamentally oppose the poisonous Catholic feedback loop of guilt, shame, and "stuff you don't talk about." But no matter what I think of the Church, standing up to talk in front of my classmates about stuttering is something I never imagined I could, or might, do.

Penn State, Part 1

L ooking at the photos, it's as if there's an invisible wall running through the center of our dorm room. On Dan's side, right up to the first inch of my side, hang companion posters of the Super Bowl–champion Steelers and an unshakable Sidney Crosby, NHL phenom, midskate. Next to Dan's bed is a WWE Divas pinup and a supersize *Maxim* cover. The bookshelf above his desk is filled with provisions: bottles of Frank's RedHot, Wish-Bone ranch dressing, a Costco-size box of Easy Mac. Then there's my side. My bed is surrounded by a brooding Bob Dylan, a *Born to Run*–era Bruce Springsteen, Jimi Hendrix's *Axis: Bold as Love* album cover, and a vintage Bob Marley poster from a 1979 gig at the Apollo, featuring a "special visual appearance" by Marcus Garvey. (By that I mean a vintage-looking reproduction I bought at the student union; it would be years before I even knew who Marcus Garvey was.)

This is Penn State summer session. It's an academic purgatory for incoming freshmen who might not have had the strongest grades in high school, though some students show up voluntarily to secure a few credits before fall semester. I'm at Penn State because I didn't have the test scores, or the GPA, to get into the University of Pennsylvania. It didn't matter

that my dad taught there, or that my brother had just graduated. I couldn't crack 500 on the math portion of my SATs,
and my reading/writing score was just okay. My college admis-
sions packet, in general, was unremarkable. I never lettered
in a varsity sport. I had written a few music reviews for *The
Hawklet,* the high school newspaper, and I had done Kairos,
but that didn't mean much to non-Jesuit schools. The truth is,
I was relieved: Penn State is nestled in the mountains between
Philadelphia and Pittsburgh, and I was ready to put some geographic distance between me and my parents. But I dreaded
the thought of sitting in class all summer while nearly everyone
I knew would be partying at the Jersey shore.

I had spent the previous summer working at a driving range/
batting cage/mini golf complex on the western edge of Philly
and had been counting on going back. It was an awful job in
so many ways, but I loved it. I'd steer an orange tractor around
the range, retrieve hundreds of golf balls, unload them into
the industrial washer, then watch them journey up a conveyor
belt and back into the vending machines. It was like a giant
game of Mouse Trap. The late shift was the best. Sometimes
friends would come by and we'd sneak a joint or a few beers
on the upper deck. I'd grab a handful of tokens so they could
hit balls for free. Unlike others, they didn't aim right at me as
I made my rounds on the range. (Nobody ever "accidentally"
hits the guy driving the ball picker.) The protective cage would
crash and shake every time a new ball made contact. To cover
the noise, I had a CD player wedged between my thigh and
the seat. I wore out Death Cab for Cutie's *Transatlanticism* that
summer. I'd climb into the tractor and lumber around the field
on methodical loops, thinking about girls who were off with
other guys.

College was a chance to reset. Dan, a blond hockey player from Pittsburgh who drove a black Ford pickup, was my randomly assigned roommate. In his Facebook profile picture, Dan was sitting around a campfire in a backward camouflage hat, making the "shocker" symbol with his mouth wide open. I concocted some elaborate excuse as to why I couldn't talk on the phone with him before we arrived.

On move-in day I stuttered horribly through introductions, then watched Dan and his mom exchange nervous glances. That afternoon, after our parents drove the few hours back to their respective sides of Pennsylvania, Dan opened his navy-blue trunk on the floor between our beds. Inside were a half dozen bottles of Admiral Nelson's spiced rum, Vladimir vodka, and several other bottom-shelf liquors. He called it his treasure chest. He surveyed the inventory and packed his lower lip with a pinch of mint-flavored Skoal. He'd plunge the brown residue into an empty Gatorade bottle with a wet *pllffffft*.

We lived on the second floor of Hartranft Hall. It was ungodly hot that summer. Dan had a tower fan next to his bed and I put a white box fan in the window that mainly blew humid air from one end of the room to the other. I bought it down at McLanahan's, the student store on College Avenue that sold can openers and condoms and rain ponchos and meatball subs and about three thousand other items. Dan and I shared a TV/DVD player combo that he brought from home. A neon Coors Light sign hummed over the dialogue of whatever TV show we'd watch. He idolized John Cena. Most weeks Dan invited guys over to scream at the TV and crush Natty Lights during *WWE Monday Night Raw*. I ended up writing a lot of papers in the computer lab.

I had two courses that summer: English 15 and Philosophy

of Art and Film. One of my classmates, Nate, a drummer from rural Elizabethtown, became a fast friend. Nate's roommate had the keys to his older brother's vacant apartment off campus. The building was largely deserted, and there was nothing in the unit except for two maroon leather couches and a plywood table with a giant graffiti tag that said, "The Bakery." Almost every day after class, we'd head there to get high. I didn't plan on becoming a college pothead. It just sort of happened when I wasn't looking.

Dan and I spent the first part of summer session mostly running in separate crowds, but one day I invited him to the Bakery. He was the type of smoker who breaks into hysterical laughter a few minutes into getting high—a full belly roar, the kind that makes everyone else laugh, too. We discovered a mutual love of Led Zeppelin, Neil Young, Pearl Jam, and many other white-guy-with-a-guitar bands. He was also a *Simpsons* aficionado. By the middle of summer he had invited me to come home with him for a weekend in Pittsburgh. Several years later I'd be one of his groomsmen.

My stutter was still omnipresent as I found my footing in college, but after three years of working with Joe and after returning from Kairos, I had stopped fighting every single block. I still couldn't bring myself to disclose the problem to others—*By the way, I stutter.* But I did begin to let myself naturally stutter through certain words and sounds, which made it much easier to finish sentences. Being away from home helped, too. There were some guys at Penn State whom I knew from high school, but 99 percent of the people I met had no knowledge of my past. A handful of frats stayed open that summer, and one in particular welcomed us in for hours of beer pong in exchange for me smoking them up. Some guys started calling me "Johnja," which I didn't love, but it was better than "Stutter Boy."

I also met a girl.

"OH MY GOD, do you remember when you met my mom?" Sam asks.

As she retells the story, her quick snort-laugh slips out. It's the first time I've heard it in over a decade. She's now married and a mom herself, living outside Philadelphia.

Sam and I first met in July 2006. It was late at night, and I was sitting on a curb eating a dollar Canyon Pizza slice next to Lloyd, a high school friend of Dan's, who would later become one of my closest college friends. As Sam walked by, she spotted the St. Joe's Prep lanyard dangling from my pocket and asked if I'd gone there. She said she had gone to an all-girls school in the area. We became inseparable that summer, but she didn't become my girlfriend until six months later. Over Christmas break, I drove to her house to meet her parents. They lived off a private road in a stately neighborhood. I parked askew in the wraparound driveway. Then I froze.

"I had told my mom: 'He's gonna come to the door, you know he's a stutterer—just pause and let him finish. Don't answer questions for him,'" Sam recalled.

"She opened the door and asked how your holidays were, and you started to stutter. She didn't even give you ten seconds. She was like, 'Oh, they were good? Oh, that's great!' She asked you four things in a row and answered all of them back-to-back-to-back. You literally couldn't answer one question. And I was upstairs just like, 'Oh my god.'"

As Sam recounted some of these memories, I realized that, no, I hadn't reached some Zen-like state of open stuttering by the time I was eighteen—I was still very much trying to hide it. Sam said that a couple of my guy friends would try to help me conceal it by finishing my sentences in group settings. And she revealed something I had always suspected but never confirmed: she'd put out little warnings before introducing me to new people.

"I would be like, 'Oh yeah, Johnny has'—I'd call you Johnny—'Johnny has a stutter, but it's fine, just don't worry about it. If he's quiet, just give him a second. He tilts his head, too, but don't worry, that's just what the stutter does.'" She said she didn't want people to think I was having a seizure. By then I was quasi-disassociating during moments of severe disfluency. I knew that my head would flail and that my eyes would hit the floor, but I tried to act normal. It was a coping mechanism that worked better some days than others. One night during freshman year, I texted a friend of a friend, asking him to come downstairs and let me into a crowded frat party. He didn't answer, so I reluctantly called him. He picked up on the third or fourth ring. Bass-heavy techno music was thumping in the background. "I put your name on the list," he shouted into the phone. "Just tell the door guy you're Stuttering John."

Sam and I lived in adjacent residence halls, so, luckily, we never had to use the phone. There were forty thousand undergrads on campus, and many of my classes were in large lecture halls where I wouldn't have to talk. Sam's older sister was a senior, and through a weird act of scheduling, she and I were in the same small lit seminar that first fall. We were regularly given writing prompts and expected to read our responses out loud. Early in the semester, when it was my turn, our professor jumped in and said, "Why don't I read this one?" I don't recall asking her to do it. I was half relieved and half embarrassed.

I asked Sam if I ever brought up my stutter when we were dating.

"You didn't seem to have an unruly amount of struggles with it," she said. "Or if you did—I don't think you really shared that."

IF YOU'RE LUCKY, you find at least one teacher who helps you see the world in Technicolor. For me it was Paul Kellermann. Paul was a musician who had performed at CBGB and other New York venues before coming to Penn State for an MFA in the late nineties. He still bobs across campus in a uniform of leather jacket, blue jeans, and Doc Martens. I sometimes think of Paul as a mix of Jeff Bridges in *The Big Lebowski* and Paul Giamatti in *Sideways:* mellow and cranky, all-knowing yet unsure.

Paul was my instructor for English 215: Introduction to Creative Nonfiction. I was a sophomore, as were most people in the room, but he treated us like grad students. The weekly reading assignments changed how I thought about writing. We'd pick apart literary journalism classics like Joan Didion's "Some Dreamers of the Golden Dream," Joseph Mitchell's "Professor Sea Gull," Terry Southern's "Twirling at Ole Miss," and Hunter S. Thompson's "The Kentucky Derby Is Decadent and Depraved." Paul also incorporated newer pieces into the syllabus, like Gary Smith's "The Man Who Couldn't Read" and Susan Orlean's "The American Male at Age 10," which made me fall in love with *Esquire.* We also wrote our own stories.

Our first assignment was to write a fifteen-hundred-word piece about an event. I filed a dispatch from an off-the-books hippie music festival on a sunflower farm about twenty-five miles outside town. There were no tickets, no vendors, and no security personnel. There was no money exchanged on the farm at all, unless you were trying to buy drugs.

Another assignment was to tell the story behind a single photograph. This was what I wrote about a three-by-five print I had hanging on the corkboard above my desk:

The picture is a vertical shot, with a slight sepia tone due to the combination of dark night and stadium halogens. There are four of us standing along a creaky metal bleacher in the SD section of Beaver Stadium. My arm is around Samantha, the brown-haired, blue-eyed girl with a teethy smile and lion paw prints on both cheeks.

Twelve hours before, my head was bobbing in a toilet as cold sweat dripped from my fingertips. I was in the middle of an unprecedented alcohol-induced sickness, one that might have ended in the emergency room had I not received her help.

I started drinking around 8 o'clock, and by 9:00 pm I knew that I was getting too drunk too quickly. Shortly after midnight I had lost my group of friends and was sitting on the couch of some older guy I knew only by association. He passed around a blunt and after three rotations I felt stuck to the couch. The combination of dizziness from drinking and heightened gravity from smoking sent me sprinting for the bathroom.

[I eventually wandered out into the night.]

A stranger in his early twenties was hovered over me trying to get my name and asking where my friends were. I couldn't answer either question, and sat with my head in my hands, watching the sidewalk spin. He yelled at me to hand him my cell phone and I struggled to get it out of my pocket. He scrolled through the recent calls and dialed the first one: Samantha.

IN THE SUMMER OF 2020, I went back to Penn State for the first time in many years. I took the long way west across Pennsylvania, listening to Built to Spill's *You in Reverse.* I still knew every crevice of the drive. I rolled past the sad windowless strip clubs and the truck stop where I used to pull off to go to the bathroom. The Red Rabbit drive-in hot dog stand was still there. I could sense all the mountain bends. I remembered the long climb up and over the peak of Bald Eagle State Forest, when my RPMs would tick up and the tractor trailers had to switch on their hazard lights. Whenever I'd hit this part of the drive, I knew that peace was waiting for me down in the valley, that I was far away from the stress and pain and resentment of home.

Paul showed up at my Airbnb in his blue Mets hat and a They Might Be Giants shirt that said "Science Is Real." For a few hours one afternoon we sat on a patio overlooking a creek, drinking and reminiscing.

"I had taught people who stutter, but not as badly as you," Paul said. "The only thing I worried about was that someone was going to interrupt you. Sometimes when you spoke, you could feel the tension rising, but I was more nervous that someone was gonna do something stupid than I was worried that you might be stuck on a word." He smiled. "Are you aware of what you look like when you do that?"

"I'm . . . aware of . . . certain characteristics," I said. "But describe it for me."

"The only way I can describe it is it's like the macaw we used to have. You would turn your head up and to the left."

He reenacted my stutter in slow motion, like a baseball coach addressing a batter's broken swing. We talked about the nature of tension, both the physical manifestation of it in my body and the invisible tension that can permeate a roomful of students.

We were thirteen years removed from English 215, and I was now a professional journalist, but sitting there with my recorder between us, scribbling notes in a green Moleskine, I still felt like I had to prove myself to him. I asked Paul if I seemed any different now than I had when he was my teacher. He wandered for a bit, then landed on a writerly phrase: "You're a more settled version of yourself."

"Is there . . . anything different about the . . . way I'm talking?"

"Well, it's weird, because we're talking about the way you're talking—so it turns into this meta thing. But you're speaking in a more assured way. Like, when you would come to my office, you'd still fall into a stutter here and there, but it was more natural, as opposed to in class, where, in many ways, it's an artificial situation. Some people are really good at it; some people need to build themselves up to say something," he said. "I was very cognizant of not putting you on the spot, but you had the best things to say."

I told him how stuttering was something I'd never really spoken about until recently, with the exception of fleeting moments like Kairos, and, in a way, suppressing this part of me really had made dealing with it easier. Now that I had started digging into my history with it, I felt like I was walking around with a giant "S" stitched to my chest—that stuttering was being transformed from an internal shame to an outward-facing scarlet letter.

"Yeah, but it's going to be," Paul said. "Whether you embrace it or not."

We talked a lot about writing. I had just finished reading David Carr's 2008 memoir, *The Night of the Gun,* a raw account of Carr's decades-long struggle with substance abuse, from alcohol to crack. Rather than work solely from his admittedly foggy memory, Carr interviews people from his past and tries to fill in some of the holes. I knew I wanted to try that. As Carr notes, it's a strange exercise. On one hand, it's an excuse to talk to people you may have long ago lost touch with (like your kindergarten teacher, or your sixth-grade girlfriend). But on the other, you're now obligated to talk to people who are still in your life about things both of you might prefer to forget. Without saying the phrase "my family," I started talking to Paul about my family.

"I was . . . lying awake at four a.m. thinking about this," I said. "If . . . Carr's book is all about memory, the imperfection of memory, I want . . . part of my book to be about . . . people versus characters. In the narrative of our lives . . . people are characters, and they're . . . good characters or bad characters. But the reality is that they're multidimensional, nuanced people, and a lot of their choices and decisions are totally . . . independent of our lives."

"I think I've probably told you this, but what you write about something—that's to cleanse your memory," Paul said. "So, bear that in mind."

12

A Hand Full of Wheel

By junior year I had started to build my portfolio of published stories. The farm festival piece I wrote for Paul's class later ran in a campus magazine, which helped me get a part-time internship at *MAGNET,* a Philly-based music magazine. I wrote blog posts and reviewed concerts for the website and put together a short profile of a psychedelic folk band, Espers, which made it to print. Still, I was rejected for internships at *The Washington Post, TIME,* the *Austin American-Statesman,* and the *Chicago Tribune.*

I applied to *The Denver Post* on a whim the night before the deadline. A couple of months later I was reading under a green desk lamp on the second floor of the library when my phone buzzed. I hurried out to the hallway and could barely say my name: "Thhhi-thiiss-is—jjjJOHN." I stuttered severely through the interview, but Ray, the paper's Arts & Entertainment editor, ignored it and told me he liked my writing voice. A few days later he offered me a full-time summer gig that paid $486 a week. I couldn't believe it.

It's eighteen hundred miles if you drive straight from Philadelphia to Denver, but we took the long way. Riding shotgun was Andy, a summer session friend who volunteered to come along for the trip then fly home. Andy had shaggy brown hair and always kept a pack of Camel Turkish Golds in his breast pocket. I had drawn up a horseshoe route through the United States, marking off cities and towns I'd romanticized from the confines of my teenage bedroom. I had a few pairs of internship-appropriate khaki pants and button-down shirts lying flat in the trunk. Nothing could stop us as we hit the road in my parents' 2003 Toyota Camry.

That first night, after a long day on I-95 South, we sat around an old friend's backyard in Richmond, Virginia, fanning the crackling flames of a pre-summer bonfire. A couple nights later we crashed with one of my Holy Trinity classmates who had moved to Athens, Georgia. We spent two nights in New Orleans, singing and laughing with elbows on the piano at Lafitte's Blacksmith Shop before shuffling off to Frenchmen Street to slip in and out of jazz clubs. We downed Lone Stars and ate chicken-fried steak in Austin, Texas. The next afternoon it felt like we were the only car on the highway for miles, zooming west across I-10, trying to make it to El Paso before dark.

There was so much of the country we hadn't seen. Andy and I streamed past fireworks stands and Waffle Houses. We were shocked to see so many Confederate flags. We drove through a biblical flood in Fort Stockton, Texas, and torrential hailstorms all along the Front Range in Colorado. I stared out the window at the desolate landscape as we made our way up I-25: Albuquerque, Santa Fe, Colorado Springs. When it was over, we had clocked 3,452 miles before pulling into Denver.

I wandered all over the city, trying to get my bearings in the place I'd soon be covering. Lindsay, one of the paper's football beat writers, let me rent a spare room in her house. It was a strange era to be at a regional newspaper. The 2008 financial crash catalyzed a depressing marathon of layoffs and buyouts and furloughs that would continue through the next decade. The *Post*'s main competitor, the *Rocky Mountain News,* had shuttered overnight just a few months before I got there. Somehow, amid all of this, the *Post* was about to win four Pulitzers in four years.

My desk was a low-walled cubicle opposite Pete, the section's grandmotherly executive assistant who cursed under her breath. Her phone rang constantly, as did the phones of all the writers and editors. If not out reporting stories in person, people mostly conducted phone interviews at their desks. I kept avoiding setting up my voicemail.

My first assignment was to write about a lost colony of geodesic domes near the state's southern border with New Mexico. Suzanne, the lifestyle editor, had dug up some dramatic black-and-white photos of the property from the paper's archives. (First lesson of newspaper journalism: any article reads stronger when placed next to great art.) Suzanne wanted me to interview two filmmakers who were working on a documentary about the settlement.

By this point I could power through in-person interviews, but I still dreaded having to pick up the phone. The documentarians were in New York. After a couple hours of stalling, I walked over to Suzanne's desk and looked anywhere but her eyes while asking if it would be a problem for me to send them questions via email. She had a son about my age, and she immediately flipped into mom mode.

"Of course that's fine," she said. "We do email interviews all the time."

I knew that wasn't true. I walked back to my desk with my head down and began typing out questions. I hadn't been at the paper a week and was already falling into the avoidance trap. I felt like I was back in high school, pointing instead of speaking. When was this going to stop? I was twenty-one years old. I was showing up to a legitimate newsroom every day. I had a reporter's notebook and pens and a little tape recorder. I was playing the part of a professional, and they were treating me like one. Why couldn't I find the courage to use the fucking phone?

I was more than a decade younger than the two youngest guys in the section, Ricardo and John. Their blue file cabinets were covered in peeling bumper stickers and festival badges. They were inundated with advance CDs from buzzy record labels. Both of them went out of their way to be nice to me, inviting me to lunches and happy hours. Ricardo knew I loved Wilco, and when the band's publicist wanted him to interview the lead singer, Jeff Tweedy, about their new record, he handed the interview off to me.

"They're gonna give you about twenty minutes on the phone with him tomorrow," Ricardo said.

I felt like I was going to throw up. Beyond the fact that I was embarrassingly starstruck, I didn't trust myself to ask smart questions with enough clarity over the phone. Tweedy was someone I had admired as both a musician and a writer since my junior year of high school. I still recite his lyrics in my head as I make my bed or do other mundane tasks. This was my chance to talk to a definitive artist about his work, for my work. But I was afraid to stutter with him on the other end of the phone. Ricardo pushed me to do it anyway.

I didn't sleep that night. When my call time rolled around the next day I retreated to the conference room so no one could hear me speak. Tweedy's voice was instantly familiar.

Hey, this is Jeff.

Hhhhuh-hey jjj-Jeff this is . . . . JOHN.

The conference room had large glass walls. Everyone could see me pacing around and straining my neck as I talked. I walked in circles around the long wood table. I scrunched the phone between my ear and my shoulder, scribbling notes as he spoke. Tweedy never reacted to my stutter. About ten minutes into the call I became more lucid—not fluent, but vaguely conversational. I stopped looking at my prewritten questions and began responding to what he was saying in real time. He gave me strong quotes, including one about how the band used to be "full of babies." I stayed at my desk past midnight writing the story, which was due the next morning. It ran on the Friday section cover above the fold. It's one of my favorite things I've ever written.

Later that summer, at the Mile High Music Festival, I wandered backstage and interviewed Patrick Carney, the drummer of the Black Keys. He was leaning against his trailer smoking a cigarette, and when he heard me stutter severely on my opening question he immediately let his guard down: "I honestly think I have tour-induced anxiety," he told me. Before the summer was over, I'd written about a John Denver impersonator, a pinball mecca, and a monthly freak show. Slowly, I was beginning to feel like a real journalist.

But why was I still so afraid of certain speaking scenarios? My editors and colleagues had accepted my disfluency. My rock idol had been okay with it. I was far from home, doing exactly what I had spent years dreaming of doing. Why did I still wince every time the phone rang? What would it take to desensitize myself to the sound of my own voice?

13

Penn State, Part 2

I had a dream recently that I was on the verge of not graduating from college. It's one I've had, in one form or another, about every two months for the past ten years. A psychologist might say that the event is merely a stand-in for whatever other anxiety currently consumes me. But really, I almost didn't graduate. My family has never known this.

I avoided taking Communication Arts and Sciences (CAS) 100, a required introductory public speaking course, term after term, year after year, until I had reached senior year with my back against the wall. My academic adviser had always tiptoed around the fact that I was putting it off. Not long ago I searched for "CAS 100" in my email archive. There are fourteen messages in the thread, and they paint a picture of my desperation. Here's one from the comms professor, Dr. Johnstone.

Dear John:
    I would be happy to meet with you to talk about alternatives to taking CAS 100, but you might want to consider the following in the meantime. One is that you take CAS 100B (Group Discussion) instead of CAS 100A (Public Speaking). CAS 100B does require

students to give one individual presentation toward the end of the semester, but not the 3–4 required in 100A. Another alternative is to try the "Credit by Examination" procedure (which involves both taking examinations, written and oral, on the textbook, and designing and presenting a speech to a group of CAS 100A instructors). I'll be glad to explain this option in more detail, if you'd like, during a conversation, but in either case you'll see that you will have to be giving at least one speech no matter which route you take. On the other hand, taking CAS 100A might still be beneficial for you, as it would give you several opportunities to practice and develop your speaking skills, and this might even help you in managing your speech impediment more effectively. Of course, the class is not one in speech therapy, but perhaps practice will be useful.

It's a very thoughtful note. I waited awhile to respond to him, and we finally met in December, right before I went home for Christmas. When I got back to campus in January, I kept avoiding registering for the class. I don't know what I was thinking. Here's an email I sent him on January 9, still trying to weasel out of it:

As all of the sections of CAS 100B are currently filled, I'm writing to suggest another alternative for fulfilling my requirement. This semester I will be TA'ing Paul Kellermann's English 215 course. I will attend every class meeting and assist Paul in lectures and discussions, as well as the usual grading papers, etc.

*Would it be possible to count this for CAS credits
if Paul were to assess my performance as an effective
instructor to determine my final course grade? Perhaps
also you or other CAS professors could sit in on a class
led by me at some point in the semester as a form of
assessment?*

Let me know what you think.

Best,

John

This was such a weak gambit. I'd never give one "lecture" in
Paul's class. I'd mostly lead small workshop groups of three or
four students at a time. Of course Dr. Johnstone wasn't going
to buy it. We were now at January 15, around the end of the
add/drop period. I was out of options. So I got the textbook
and essentially did the class as an independent study. I barely
passed the first written exam. I delayed trying to put together
my big speech until the last possible weekend of spring semester. Here are some Gchats with my friend Allison from that May.
We're now two weeks away from graduation.

ALLISON: are you going to come to my parteeee
ME: is there such an appropriate answer as maybe
ALLISON: ya
ALLISON: maybe is okay
ME: ok, maybe
ME: i have a 15 pager between now and friday
ME: and an exam friday
ME: and a speech to give next tuesday
ALLISON: blech

ME: shitty situation
ALLISON: tuesday? wtf

[Tuesday was *after* the conclusion of finals week.]

ME: yeah. im doing it as credit-by-exam so its outside the
     context of a classroom
ME: but still gotta do it in order to get that diploma next
     saturday
ALLISON: i dont understand
ALLISON: for your TA position or what?
ME: CAS 100
ME: the bane of my existence
ALLISON: ugh
ME: its like
ME: i cant even explain it
ME: its like a bully holding your head under water

Many of my senior classmates were stumbling around town on bar tours while I was in my apartment trying to practice the speech. When Tuesday came, I trudged to the vacant comms building, where Dr. Johnstone and a handful of his colleagues were waiting for me. The assignment was to speak persuasively about one issue—I chose state-level marijuana legalization.

I walked to the front of the room, shaking. It was supposed to be a ten-minute monologue, but I was out of breath by the end of the first sentence. The speech took me well over half an hour. I barely looked one of them in the eye, focusing instead on the rattling paper near my waist. I didn't project. I couldn't produce one fluent sentence. I was never able to steady my airflow or my heart rate. When it was over, Dr. Johnstone told me to wait in an adjacent classroom.

Graduation was just four days away. If you didn't meet the final requirements, you could put on a cap and gown and walk across the stage, but you'd receive a blank diploma. I was mentally preparing myself for this outcome but horrified at the thought of having to explain everything that had happened to my parents, and of having to do CAS 100 over again in the summer. I sat down at a desk in the empty room and felt cool sweat in every crevice of my body. When Dr. Johnstone came in, he put his hands out and patted the air—the classic "calm down" motion.

"You passed," he said. "Just barely—but you passed."

14

"Sir! What Language Do You Speak?"

I figured I'd stay in my college apartment until the lease ended in mid-August, though I didn't have much of a plan besides that.

I burned a week couch-surfing in New York and watched the Fourth of July fireworks with old friends in D.C., but most days I'd wake up and scour Craigslist for writing jobs in far-flung places, sending my résumé and cover letter into the void. I'd take long, aimless drives around the farmlands surrounding campus. I'd stay up until four or five in the morning writing little essays in a notebook that I'd eventually throw away. Some days I worked as a fill-in barista at a hookah lounge/head shop/coffeehouse called Chronic Town, and the owners gave me intermittent shifts at their short-lived record store down the street. In a way, this was a fulfillment of a lifelong dream. I was the guy on the stool behind the raised counter, pretending to know everything about every band. Never mind that most shifts I'd barely serve any customers.

Most of my friends had left town. I started hanging out with Allison's old roommates at 501 West College Avenue, a massive orange-brick house that had been divided into apartments. On any night of the week, 501's long front porch would be filled with five to ten people drinking, smoking, listening to music, and waxing poetic about college life. Friends and quasi-friends would wander up to the porch with some sort of booze as an offering and pull up a chair or lean against the railing. I'd ride my bike over with a twelve-pack of Extra Gold, the cheapest beer at Brewsky's Bottle Shop, balancing on the handlebars. I did much more listening than talking those nights. People volleyed in conversation at a pace that I admired but couldn't keep up with. Sometimes I would chime in with a stray thought about music. That porch was the first place I heard Television's "Marquee Moon," which instantly became one of my all-time favorite songs.

Allison comes from a music-loving family. Her little brother, Justin, is a talented guitar player and songwriter. He's also a person who stutters, but she and I had never really talked about that until I started writing this book.

"When we were kids, it was always a point of teasing, like a really low blow," Allison told me. "You know, like, 'At least I don't stutter' or 'W-w-w-what did you say, Justin?' We definitely didn't toss that around lightly; it was only used when we were really mad at each other."

She became a little squeamish when talking about Justin's bar mitzvah, when he had to stand and read from the Torah in front of roughly a hundred people at the family's synagogue outside Philadelphia.

"I was a senior in high school and he was in seventh grade. I remember feeling secondhand embarrassment and anxiety, and people seeming kind of impatient. It was hard for him to sound confident, you know? And he still did it. He got through it. He's a really confident man now."

A couple weeks later, when I asked Justin about that day, he told me that it was a traumatizing experience.

"You spend months preparing for your bar or bat mitzvah, all the prayers, all the things that you read or chant. I had a tutor for it, and I definitely didn't stutter as much with just them. But when I was in front of all these people, it just—that destroyed everything," he said. "As soon as I was done, it was like this huge weight was lifted off my shoulders. I never want to have to think about that again."

These days Justin makes solo music. He's worked as a professional engineer at Sear Sound, a legendary recording studio in Manhattan. He told me about crossing paths at a festival with a guitarist named Lyle Brewer, who also stutters. "I would love for you to talk to him," Justin said.

EVEN BEFORE I MET Lyle Brewer, I wanted one of his T-shirts. He sells a variety of styles, but the most popular is jet-black with nine lines of white text running across the front. His name pops in bright red. It looks like this:

Luh, Luh, Luh, Luh, Luh,
Luh, Luh, Luh, Luh,
Lyle
Buh, Buh, Buh, Buh, Buh,
Buh, sorry, Buh, Buh, Buh,
Brew, Brew, wuh,
wuh, damnit,
Buh, Buh, Buh,
Brewer

He sells the stutter shirts for twenty-five bucks apiece, mainly through Instagram. He'll occasionally alert his followers to a new shipment, and they tend to disappear fast. Reading the text aloud can make you feel like you're trapped in a long period of disfluency. But when you pull back to look at the whole shirt, there's an inherent musicality to the graphic. The lines almost look like a poem—or lyrics to a song. When you produce the sounds in quick succession, you'll notice the "Luh" and "Buh" are deep and rhythmic, like the tone on a bass guitar. The "wuh" stutters that appear after "Brew" resemble the onomatopoeia of a wah-wah pedal, the piece of equipment that helps guitarists bend and stretch notes beyond their traditional limitations. (Think of the psychedelic version of "The Star-Spangled Banner" that Jimi Hendrix performed during the final hours of Woodstock.)

"That shirt is kind of me getting back at all the frustration that I have at not being able to speak the way I want to," Lyle told me. "I think it was just a way of, like, telling everyone, so I don't have to go through any more of this shit."

He has a naturally warm voice and speaks with a weathered croak. His stutter can fluctuate from nonexistent to omnipresent. When he's stuck on a vowel, he tries to release the tension in his mouth by drooping and wiggling his jaw, giving the word room to eventually glide out, even if that means he's holding up conversation for a couple of extra seconds. He has deep blue eyes that flutter slightly when he elongates words and phrases, especially ones that begin with the letter "s." When this happens, his gaze tends to drift off to the left, though he doesn't telegraph that he's uncomfortable. Lyle's stutter is less of a violent event exploding out of his body and something more akin to a hummingbird, or a calm vibration.

"I think the hardest part is pretending that it's not there," he said. "I don't know—it's funny. It *does* sound unusual. And I can't not acknowledge the fact that it's really uncomfortable.

It sounds kind of jarring. And if people don't know it's coming, it's really confusing."

Lyle speaks about stuttering like no one else I've met. He's searingly honest about his ambivalence toward the role it plays in his life.

"I joke around that stuttering is, like, the least useful adaptation ever created," he said. "That whole argument 'Whatever doesn't kill you makes you stronger,' I think that's the biggest pile of horseshit ever. I hate that. I've had stuttering phone calls for thirty years and they're not getting any easier. And it's not like I go through my thousandth one and then all of a sudden I'm much stronger. It's—it's not getting better," he said. "And I'm trying, man."

Lyle is an acclaimed guitarist who has toured internationally with multiple bands. When he's not on the road, he works as an assistant professor of guitar at Berklee College of Music. His stutter is one of the reasons he's dedicated his life to mastering an art form he can practice with his hands. Most of Lyle's waking hours are devoted to composing complicated instrumental medleys in his lofted rehearsal space. It's a simple room on the top floor of his home with low ceilings, a beige carpet, and about a dozen guitars, plus amplifiers, pedals, microphones, and other equipment. Most days he shares short instructional videos from this room with his thousands of Instagram followers. He often stutters as he explains the notes he's playing. There's no one else in there, but that doesn't matter—he'll still break eye contact with the camera lens out of habit.

Watching, and listening, to Lyle play the guitar is a mesmerizing experience. His fingers dance up and down the neck, stretching across multiple frets, creating a sound that is clean and elegant. His music is contemplative but not meandering.

His compositions sometimes appear to be telling a story that he doesn't want to say out loud. Another shirt he sells reads, "Sticks and Stones May Break My Bones But Words Will Never Be In Any Lyle Brewer Songs." It's a nod to the fact that, even though he plays in traditional rock and roll bands, everything he creates as a solo artist is instrumental. His songs are so beautifully constructed that words might even diminish their value.

"I really like playing music because I can be as free as I want to, and I can say whatever I want, and I don't have to be interrupted and constantly reminded of the fact that I'm different," he said.

For a while, Lyle would post photos of his Starbucks orders with wrong names on the side of the cup: Kyle, Lionel, Lloyd. Once, when out shopping for new clothes, a clerk called out to him from across the store, asking if she could help him find anything. He attempted to say no, but he blocked severely and couldn't say anything at all. "She thought I was, like, having a heart attack or something," Lyle said. "She was like, 'Sir, is everything okay?' That made me stutter even worse, where I looked like I was having a seizure or some shit. She was like, 'Sir! Sir! What language do you speak?'"

If he introduces himself to someone and they give him The Look, he may not speak again as long as the two of them are in the same room. Occasionally he'll walk away from a social situation to briefly cry and then compose himself. "One of the things that sucks about going on tour is you meet people all the time," he said. The emcee at a music venue once approached Lyle and asked him how to pronounce his name so she could introduce him onstage. As you're reading this, try to enunciate the word "Brewer" out loud. The opening "Br" sound has to connect with the middle "ew" before you reach the final "er." Those dueling "r" sounds are not very common in English. You may notice that your lips bounce, and that the muscles under your chin momentarily tighten up. If you're a person who stutters, you may block on the opening "b" or have trouble forming the "br" cluster at the front of your mouth. Lyle's name has haunted him his entire life—as it did that night with the emcee at the club.

"I said, 'Br-r-r-ruh—Bruh-ew-ewer,' and she said it back to me exactly the way I said it. And I looked at her, and I was just like, 'You've got to be kidding me.'" He was half laughing, half cringing.

"It feels like I'm working really hard for something that doesn't mean very much," he said. "If I wanna say, 'That show we played was in Duh-duh-Durham,' and there's five people around who don't know I have a speech impediment, then I'm not gonna struggle through a sentence at the risk of being really embarrassed, or because of the physical discomfort of talking," he said. "People who don't stutter don't understand how much strategy is involved, and how much, like, self-preservation there is."

Lyle has a son, Elliott, who is now in middle school and has been finding his way around the guitar. Lyle's face changes as he watches his son noodle on the instrument. His cheekbones rise and his eyes widen as Elliott plucks his way through classics like "Back in Black," "Here Comes the Sun," and "Wish You Were Here." Sometimes they'll practice together, and Lyle is careful not to correct his son's mistakes, though he's always ready with a celebratory fist bump or high five. Unlike most stutterers I've spoken with, Lyle doesn't mind if people try to finish his sentences, especially his son. "If I'm trying to say something and someone wants to do detective work and tag-team a word with me, I'm like, great, that's awesome."

Reading out loud is especially hard for Lyle. When Elliott was three years old, he began to help his dad when he noticed him stutter. "Sometimes with Dr. Seuss, where it's, like, nonsense word after nonsense word, I'm, like, busting my ass," he said with a laugh. "When he was really into dinosaurs, I'd be trying to pronounce these long-ass names."

LYLE AND I HAD BEEN in touch for almost a full year before we finally met in person. One summer day I drove to his place not far from Boston. He stuttered like hell when I first arrived. I blocked hard, too, and made a nervous joke about two stutterers being trapped in purgatory. I closed the front door and followed him upstairs to his apartment. He has the top two floors of an old white house on a quiet street. There were boxes of vinyl records stacked in the living room alongside the stutter shirts.

Lyle grabbed two cans of seltzer and led me to his back porch. Mosquitoes flew around our ankles. He was partially shaven, barefoot, and his tattoos were visible through his yellow T-shirt. A mop of brown hair poked out of his Red Sox hat. We sat side by side in plastic folding chairs and talked, sometimes looking at each other, mostly looking off into the distance. His face contains a lot of lived experience. He looked tired but not exhausted. There's palpable soul in his eyes.

There was a pizza on the kitchen counter, half cheese, half pepperoni, that he had picked up not long before I got there. It was a thoughtful gesture; he joked about how becoming a dad had taught him all that stuff. His girlfriend, Georgia, was working at a table in a little room off the kitchen and Elliott was finishing up the last week of remote school in his room.

Lyle talked about the economics of having a small, devoted fan base versus playing as a sideman in some other person's band. He was noodling on a beautiful sunburst guitar in the living room when Elliott joined us. Lyle handed him the guitar and taught him to play Neil Young's "Harvest Moon." Elliott has a toothy, honest smile like his dad.

A bucket of baseballs was sitting in the corner of the living room. I picked one up and started tossing it, and Elliott told me about his team. Lyle said that, during the early games of the season, he had mostly stared at his shoes on the sidelines, not making an effort to socialize with the other parents, but by the end of the year he had found the courage to go over and talk. I grabbed an old black Spalding glove and began throwing the ball into the pocket to get that satisfying *smack*. Lyle asked Elliott to grab the other gloves so the three of us could go outside and play catch. Elliott's face lit up and he offered me a piece of gum on our way out the door. We threw the ball around in a little triangle for a while, not really talking, not really needing to. Then a summer storm blew in and we hustled up the back steps into the kitchen.

Lyle showed me pictures of him and his brother in baseball uniforms back when they were little kids. He pointed to images of his parents, and a framed photo of himself playing onstage a decade ago. I thought back to that first day he and I talked the previous summer. As we daydreamed about living another life where neither of us stuttered, Lyle was especially lucid and became almost perfectly fluent for sentences at a time. He told me he would sell every item he owned if he could have surgery to make his stutter go away.

"I would love the ability to go around and say hi to people and not feel like the world was going to end," he said. "And I would love to communicate with whoever I wanted to, and speak exactly how I wanted to, and make people happy, and be able to, like, participate in the thing that everybody does so freely, and I would have such appreciation for the spoken word that I wouldn't want to miss out on what that feels like, because I thought about what it would be like for so long. I would be funny and I would be caring and I would be articulate, and I would learn a fuck ton of new words just so I could say them whenever I wanted to. I would take up public speaking just 'cause I could, 'cause I would be so happy. I would talk to every single person I saw on the street. I would, you know, like, I don't know—I would make five-hour-long Facebook Live videos where I'd just read the dictionary or some shit like that."

He laughed as he rattled off hypothetical after hypothetical.

"You try to tell whatever side of the story you're feeling at that time," he said later. "Either that you're overcoming it or it's, like, killing you. You don't ever get to tell both. And I think that's a more complete picture. Like, I am trying to overcome it, and it is kind of killing me. But the reality is, it's not actually killing me, and I'm not really overcoming it."

15

One-Way West

Midsummer, 2010. I told my parents that if I was still unem-ployed come September, I'd move to New Orleans and become a bartender. This seemed like a great idea on paper; never mind the fact that I had zero bartending experience and still wasn't entirely comfortable talking to strangers.

I had been emailing back and forth with Ray, my old editor at *The Denver Post,* about a potential full-time gig at the paper. They were turning their music blog, *Reverb,* into a stand-alone website and looking for someone to run it. In late July I flew out to Colorado to interview for the position. I was running out of days before I'd have to turn over the keys to my Penn State apartment. In August, when the lease finally ended, I packed everything I owned into the back of my trunk and drove home, wondering when I'd have enough money to actually start a life as an adult.

Forty-eight hours later, Ray called: I had the job. I ran to the backyard to tell my mom. Her face was a mix of excitement and heartbreak. Even though she was thrilled for me, she kept talk-ing about how Colorado was so far away. My dad had moved around a lot as a young reporter and knew that this is how it goes: you find an opening at a paper, you take it; where it is on the map doesn't really matter. I left home four days later.

This time my friend Kev came along to ride shotgun. Kev and I had met a couple of years earlier when I spent a week in New York covering the CMJ Music Marathon for a small blog. I had posted on Facebook that I was looking for a place to stay, and Doc, one of my brother's college friends, offered me his couch. Doc didn't mention that he wouldn't be there—and that he lived with someone else. That first night, his roommate, Kev, came home at two a.m. and had no idea who this stranger was in his living room. I stuttered through an awkward introduction and he instantly welcomed me in. Every night that week we bounced around downtown Manhattan. I was underage and didn't have a fake ID, but he showed me how to carry myself to get past the door guys. Back at his apartment late at night, we'd climb through the kitchen window to sit on the fire escape. We'd smoke and drink and talk until the early morning hours. We stayed in close touch after I left. Doc eventually moved down to Austin, but I kept taking trips up to New York just to hop around the city with Kev. When I told him my news about the Denver job, without a moment's hesitation he said, "Cool, I'll drive out there with you."

On a Saturday morning in late August, we headed west. My parents had helped me buy a used Jeep a few years earlier. The air conditioner was broken, so we drove the whole way with the windows down. That first night we pulled into a motel outside Cleveland and stumbled across the parking lot to an empty Buffalo Wild Wings. We made it to Chicago early the next afternoon and caught a Cubs game at Wrigley Field. On a rainy Monday night in Omaha, we ate colossal steaks and downed whiskey drinks at Mr. Toad's Pub. The next morning was a seemingly endless drive across the Nebraska plains, stopping for snacks and gas whenever a Sinclair long-neck dinosaur would appear. Kev kept saying how surreal it was that I was driving only *one way*. It was something I had dreamed about since childhood, just getting in the car and leaving. I wasn't scared. I wasn't sad.

We pulled into Denver on Tuesday night and took a good-bye photo in front of the car. Looking at it now, it's one of the happiest images I've ever seen of myself. I'm in a white V-neck undershirt and jeans, smiling with my whole face. Kev is grinning and looking off-camera, one thumb on the filter of an unlit cigarette. The next morning, I dropped him off at the airport so he could fly home to New York, then I started searching for a place to live.

Ricardo, the paper's music critic, lent me his couch for a few days as I scouted apartments. Two miles south of downtown I rode past a huge Victorian house that had been converted into apartments. The front half of the first floor was available for six hundred dollars a month. It was perfect. The only catch was that it was under construction and wouldn't have running water until October. I left this part out when I called home to tell my parents the good news. I soon started sleeping at the new place, even though I couldn't shower or use the sinks. I bought a big bottle of hand sanitizer and a jug of Poland Spring to brush my teeth. Every morning I'd wake up early and head to work to shower in the employee locker room, hoping none of my new colleagues would see me.

I had picked up some of the rhythms of adulthood during my internship the previous summer, but now I was really on my own. I stuttered through exhausting automated phone calls to set up internet service and waited in an interminable DMV line for a Colorado driver's license. On Saturday mornings I'd walk to the Goodwill store on South Broadway and look for furniture in the basement. I found a wobbly nightstand and a handsome wood bed frame with a Grateful Dead sticker on the headboard for about thirty bucks. Week by week, month by month, I started putting a life together.

Everyone I met out west seemed nicer and more patient with my stutter. The first question you'd hear wasn't "So, what do you do?" Nobody really cared where you'd gone to school or who your parents were. So many Denverites were transplants from other parts of the country. Many of the people I was meeting had left a job or fallen out with their family and had moved to Colorado looking for a fresh start. Strangers would invite you outside to smoke weed after a few minutes of chatting at the bar. People you barely knew would ask you to go hiking or camping with them.

I became a regular at Sputnik, a hipster bar next to a tiny rock club called the Hi-Dive. I'd sit in the corner by the window with a basket of french fries and a pint of PBR, occasionally chatting with the bartenders. A few blocks farther down Broadway was the Skylark Lounge, a rockabilly bar with checkered floors and vintage movie posters. The second floor had pristine Brunswick pool tables, shuffleboard, and old pinball machines. Tom, the upstairs bartender, always greeted me by name with a firm handshake whenever I'd take a seat at the curved counter. I'd walk home from the Skylark late at night, smoke a joint, and stare at the moon. I didn't mind being so far from everything and everybody I knew. I felt more like myself than I had in a while.

At work, I was by far the youngest person in the Features section. But now that I was no longer an intern, the other writers and editors treated me like a peer. I started out writing "furniture" for the Friday section—little blocks of text to fill out the page around longer feature stories. Most of these assignments were small previews of concerts and other local events, though my main job was to write, edit, and publish multiple posts per day on the music blog, *Reverb*.

So, yeah, the job: wake up every day and cover music. What more could a twenty-two-year-old want? During my first year at the paper, I saw shows four or five nights a week. If I wasn't out hearing live music, I was obsessively reading. I subscribed to *Esquire* and would lie on my couch with the windows open, studying the masthead, ingesting each issue cover to cover the day it arrived, just like I used to with *SPIN* and *Rolling Stone*. On Sundays I'd ride my bike to the Tattered Cover bookstore and flip through the first-floor racks. I'd pull down *New York* magazine, *The New Yorker, Vanity Fair,* and *The Atlantic* and take a seat while the hours flew by. I was mesmerized by the feature stories and tried to deconstruct them.

Ray could eventually tell that I was getting restless with my focus on music. Early on, he started entertaining my pitches for little essays to run in the Friday and Sunday sections. I did a piece about the release of *The Social Network* and coming of age online—all those long nights on AIM, trying to be a cooler version of myself. I wrote about the way Colorado businesses treated massive 4/20 events and about the rapid gentrification of my neighborhood as told through the prism of Badger's Pub, the "last true dive bar." I also tried to say something about more serious topics like the Jerry Sandusky scandal at Penn State and the Tucson shooting. Some of these pieces worked better than others.

During my second year at the *Post,* the paper's parent company, MediaNews Group, was sold to an East Coast hedge fund, and two different newspaper chains were set to converge under an aspirational banner, Digital First Media. We learned that the new CEO was starting a national office in Manhattan to manage all of the properties, and that his team would be hiring about fifty journalists to run the centralized operation. It was more of a back-room, bureaucratic gig than I'd ever imagined myself pursuing, but it was also a full-time job in New York. I used to sit at my desk in Denver and type various search terms into my browser: "West Village," "Lower East Side," "Williamsburg," daydreaming. I was offered one of the new jobs in October 2012. The pay was almost twice what I was making in Colorado; I said yes without negotiating. This all happened about ten days before my brother got married.

MY SISTER-IN-LAW, JENNIE, is one of the best human beings I've ever met. She's changed my brother's life, and my family's life, in immeasurable ways. I was absolutely thrilled when she said yes to my brother's proposal. I was—and remain—profoundly happy for them.

But I often return to a photo from their wedding day. My family is standing on the front steps of Holy Trinity Church, on the same block where Matt and I went to elementary school. My brother, dad, and I are wearing boxy white jackets and billowy black tuxedo pants. (My dad looks like he should be crooning Sinatra covers on a cruise ship.) Whenever I pull up this picture, I zoom in on my face. My eyes are heavy. My lips are pursed. I'm looking into the photographer's lens, but my mind is off somewhere else. I don't look sad—it's a more complicated expression than that. It's the look that washes over someone's face when they realize they can't fake it anymore. I can barely summon a half smile.

Moving to Colorado had been a way to temporarily escape

my family baggage. And, while I couldn't wait to get to New York, I was nervous about the prospect of returning to the East Coast. My brother was settled in D.C.; my parents were outside Philadelphia. They visited each other regularly. In my eyes, my mom, my dad, and Matt were happy to just shake the Etch A Sketch and erase the years of bullying and explosions. Remember, this is what Catholic families do: forget the problem, ignore it, never talk about it, smile. It seemed to be working for them. I was guilty of this behavior, too. I'd sit around the living room with everyone else on Christmas, nodding and grinning. But as soon as I'd leave I'd feel like a fraud, like I was lying to myself. That's how I look in that wedding photo.

Several hours after that picture was taken, various friends and family members rose to speak and salute the newlyweds at the reception. I remained seated, scratching the label off my bottle of beer. I watched as Jennie and her maid of honor—her younger sister—embraced at the microphone after a tender toast. Understandably, Matt had asked his friend Mark to be his best man, and he did a wonderful job with his speech.

I was a groomsman, but I never spoke during the ceremony, and I never said a word during the reception. I stared into the silverware as more guests gave toasts. I thought about how I had used my impending move as an excuse to skip his bachelor party. I drank. I fantasized about one day showing my brother all that I was still lugging around.

16

Borrowed Time

One belongs to New York instantly, one belongs to it as much in five minutes as in five years." I came across this Tom Wolfe quote a week after Matt's wedding, as I packed up my life in Denver and headed east. E. B. White once wrote that people leave small towns and go to New York to avoid "the indignity of being observed." That one really gets me. I landed in the city two days after Hurricane Sandy hit. Much of Lower Manhattan was partially blacked out, its residents trying to put their lives back together. New York felt like home from the moment I touched down at LaGuardia. There was no adjustment period; this was the life that made sense. All of it. Instantly.

If you stood in the middle of my first New York apartment, you could practically touch both walls. It was a second-floor studio above d.b.a., a dark and damp neighborhood bar on First Avenue in the East Village. The building's front door was foggy and scratched and covered in white graffiti. The interior hallways were caked in a thick layer of black grime. My neighbor, who had lived there for decades, told me how trucks drove up the block carrying wreckage from the World Trade Center after 9/11, leaving many of the brick façades coated in dust for years afterward. Someone upstairs used to hurl handfuls of birdseed onto the roof, summoning a flock of pigeons every morning. No matter the time of year, my windowsill and fire escape were drenched in that white-bluish-green hue of bird shit that looks like a custom Bob Ross color. I had a tiny bathroom with a sink and elevated shower; the toilet was tucked into a closet off the kitchen. It was strange. It was mine. I loved it.

I had downsized most of my Denver possessions and packed what remained into a large plywood box with an orange-vinyl cover that U-Haul shipped across the country. It was scheduled to arrive early on a Sunday morning. Kev was still living in the city and had offered to help me move, but he didn't want to worry about waking up early to get to my apartment, so we stayed out until last call Saturday night, then slept on the hardwood floor in my empty unit. Kev wrapped himself in a shower curtain I had picked up that day at the Astor Place Kmart. I slept on a bath towel. We woke up hungover and sat in the empty space for nine hours, waiting for the box to arrive. Andrew was also living in New York, and he had come down midday to join us. Around eight o'clock that night, when my stuff finally arrived, the guy driving the truck pried the box open with a crowbar and we carried everything up the slanted stairwell in about fifteen minutes.

The only item that broke during my move was my record player. It had been a Christmas gift from my dad during my senior year of college. One night after work I popped into Gimme Gimme Records on East Fifth Street and asked the clerk if he knew a repairman. He offered to sell me a turntable in the corner for seventy-five dollars. It was a used Technics SL-1200 with a few replacement parts and switches, but it worked perfectly. These exact record players sometimes go for two thousand dollars or more on eBay. He also gave me a mixed box of fifty or so used vinyls for five bucks. He was closing shop in a few days and moving to California. This was just my second week in the city.

The East Village had been decidedly "over" for about a decade before I got there, but I was twenty-four, so what did that matter? I stuttered everywhere, all the time, but people in New York didn't pity me the way they seemed to in D.C. or Philadelphia. I'd take a seat at the counter inside B&H Dairy on Second Avenue and try to force out "breakfast special." Even there, a cramped and chaotic hole-in-the-wall where you're on top of every other customer, the two counter guys just kept doing their thing as I struggled to talk. They didn't care that it took me a while to say "sss-s-s-suh-scrambled." I can still hear the hiss of the griddle, the scrape of the spatula, the whisk whipping against the bowl. The B&H breakfast combo remains one of the best deals in the city: seven dollars for eggs and home fries and a mini orange juice and a paper plate of buttered challah, plus all-you-can-drink coffee. I felt utterly content sitting there, eavesdropping on conversations, flipping through *The Village Voice*.

On Tuesday nights after work I'd hop off the subway and head to the readings at KGB Bar on East Fourth Street. I'd climb the steps and take a seat at one of the candlelit tables while writers I admired read their work. These were bylines I recognized from *Slate* or *The Awl* or some other in-crowd publication I had no idea how to break into. A small desk lamp illuminated their pages on an old wooden lectern. Most of them knew how to be funny, how to command a room, how to hit strategic beats so as to give life to a manuscript. On the walk home, I'd imagine myself behind the mic, looking out at tables of peers who were looking back at me with respect.

Saturdays were for dry turkey clubs and soggy fries at Odessa on Avenue A. Then I'd sit on a bench in Tompkins Square Park with a stack of magazines. At dusk I'd pop into Academy Records or Other Music and flip through the cheap stuff, and later that night I'd catch the L train at First Avenue and ride it one stop across the river to Bedford Avenue in Brooklyn. There was a trio of DIY venues across the street from the old Domino Sugar Refinery—Glasslands, 285 Kent, and Death By Audio—that hosted some of the best live shows in the city. For ten or fifteen bucks you could squeeze into loud, dirty, poorly ventilated rooms and see indie bands like Parquet Courts, Bass Drum of Death, Shannon and the Clams, and Sonny and the Sunsets. A guy I knew from college lived in the workshop/art space behind the Death By Audio stage. To get there you'd walk through a strange hallway. Behind one door was a huge industrial room with a cargo net hanging from the ribbed metal ceiling. One of the makeshift bedrooms was hidden behind a heavy rotating bookshelf like something out of 1960s *Batman*. He took me and another friend up to the roof one night to smoke and drink and enjoy the panoramic view of Manhattan. *VICE* eventually moved in and kicked everyone out.

MY SECOND DAY at my new job was Election Night 2012. Our downtown office was still closed because of Sandy, so we piled into the old Associated Press headquarters near Penn Station for a long night of . . . something. It wasn't exactly clear what we were supposed to do. We were essentially a routing station for sharing content across the company's seventy-five newspapers. All I remember from Election Night was the stack of pizza boxes from nearby NY Pizza Suprema, which became my favorite slice in the city.

Our real office was on the newly renovated twenty-fifth floor of 5 Hanover Square, near the southern tip of Manhattan. Each morning I'd get off the subway at Wall Street and walk past finance guys who looked much more put together than I did, though not necessarily happier. A big part of my job involved figuring out what entertainment articles—movie reviews, album reviews, award-show coverage—we could syndicate across the organization's newspapers. This required a lot of conference calls with other editors around the country.

I dreaded these dial-ins more than anything. I never had the courage to disclose my problem at the beginning of the call—*By the way, I stutter*—I just tried and failed to hide it. I don't recall my new boss ever asking me anything about why I talked this way and why I turned orangey red every time a new meeting would start. Sometimes one of the editors would ask if they should call back another time. I never knew what to say. So I'd just keep sweating and say nothing, then repeat the pattern again the next day.

I was in love with New York and didn't regret my decision to move, but the job was soul crushing. We were essentially trying to eliminate redundancies at these already struggling papers where journalists worked long hours for small paychecks. *The Denver Post,* one of the bigger papers in the chain, had long relied on high-priced print ads from car dealerships and mattress stores, but in the 2010s these local businesses were becoming savvier with social media and moving that ad money to Facebook. The papers kept shrinking in size, page count, and staff. Meanwhile my team was trying to justify its existence. We were writing buzzwords like "innovation" and "streamline" and "centralize" on Post-it notes to hang on glass walls. Within six months I had already started applying elsewhere.

That first winter I spent a lot of time in the Rose Reading Room at the New York Public Library trying to come up with freelance story ideas. Each Wednesday I'd pitch the music editor at *The Village Voice* and get no response. I landed one story at *Salon* only to have it killed shortly before publication. I wrote a few small album reviews for *Paste* that paid twenty-five bucks apiece. Meanwhile, I kept sending out my résumé and hearing nothing. It didn't matter that I was now a city dweller. I still felt shut out of the New York media bubble. The talent pool was so big, and everyone knew one another, or pretended like they did. None of the real magazine editors knew or cared what Digital First Media was.

Most Sunday mornings I'd zigzag across Manhattan with a copy of *The New York Times* performatively wedged under my right arm. I'd slip in and out of coffee shops, discarding completed sections of the paper for another customer to read. As I made my way home, I'd walk along Tenth Street, peering into the windows of the stately ivy-covered town houses. If it was warm, I'd park myself on one of the benches that line the cobblestone square in front of St. Mark's Church in-the-Bowery. Several years later, another stutterer would walk past those same benches and enter the church. Hundreds of people would be huddled inside, and none of them knew what was about to happen as he began to speak.

"I Kind of Leave My Body"

On January 1, 2020, JJJJJerome Ellis woke up sick in his Brooklyn apartment. He had been scheduled to perform as part of an annual New Year's Day marathon reading at St. Mark's—the same East Village church where Patti Smith first performed in 1971. Ellis had spent weeks writing and rehearsing a two-minute monologue. He had walked the streets of New York reciting his lines out loud, trying to master the beats and rhythm of the text. Now the day had arrived and he could barely move.

"I assumed there would be a few hundred people there," he later told me. "I was like, 'If there's one person in the audience who stutters, or their family member stutters, and they are helped by [what I have to say] then it will have been worth it,' you know?"

Ellis powered through his fatigue and took an Uber across the East River and up through Lower Manhattan. He got out at the church and walked through the cast-iron gates into the light-filled sanctuary. Dozens of artists would perform that day. When it was Ellis's turn, he took his place behind the lectern and gripped the microphone with both hands. He was wearing a white turtleneck and looked angelic. Within the opening seconds, he began to stutter. Audience members couldn't tell if the interruptions were intentional or not. The venue was overtaken with a heavy, intense silence as Ellis repeatedly lingered in prolonged blocks. His two-minute recitation would take him over ten minutes to complete. But the room was captivated. Seven months later, a clip of his performance would be broadcast to millions of listeners on an episode of *This American Life*.

"It gives me chills to think about, because there were those two paths," he said, acknowledging that he could have stayed in bed that morning. Scores of listeners have written to him explaining how the radio segment touched their lives. A psychotherapist near Seattle told him that she was working with a man on the autism spectrum who was struggling to process his thoughts, and that hearing Ellis describe the experience of blocking gave her a new idea for how to reach her patient. By moving their appointment to the final session of the day, the patient soon felt less performance pressure and started to open up about his problems. "The root message is not just about stuttering," Ellis told me. "It's about time."

What he read on New Year's Day was a meditation on rules that are meant to be equalizers and often become something else. His voice changed as he read this last part:

When I was first invited to participate in this magnificent event, I was struck by the two-minute time limit. Which later became a two-to-three-minute time limit. And I understood intuitively that the purpose of this time limit was to create as nonhierarchical a space as possible. But in removing one hierarchy, the time limit introduces another. A time limit assumes that all people have relatively equal access to time through their speech, which is not true. Stuttering is very unpredictable. I can rehearse something as many times as I want, but I don't actually know how long it will take me to say something until I have to say it.

Ellis is a multitalented artist. He's a gifted essayist and poet. He's also a composer with mastery of the piano, saxophone, and several other instruments, but his music doesn't fall into standard genres like classical or jazz. "So much of my work has a core motivation, which is to restore my dignity, and to restore dignity to other people who speak disfluently, or who are marginalized in some way," he told me.

He has reclaimed the power of his stutter like no one I've ever met. A couple of years ago, Ellis began spelling his first name with five "j's"—JJJJJerome—to visually depict his own disfluency. When composing new music, he often turns to drones, elongated sounds with no discernible beginning or end. He started doing this because sometimes he'll feel himself stutter while playing the saxophone, and this way it doesn't matter if he blocks on the first note.

Sometimes his art folds in on itself: one of Ellis's pieces is a video of him listening to a recording of his New Year's Day performance while transcribing his own stutter, holding down one letter on the keyboard during his blocks for lines at a time. In the video, it looks like Pac-Man zooming across the screen.

"Part of my goal in the performance was to invite the audience into the space of the block and hold the space open," he said. "I could have evaded the block in many, many ways. I could have used a synonym, or I could have rephrased something on the spot, which is something I do, of course, in my daily life." He opted to read each word exactly as he had memorized it. He told me he wanted to let his blocks exist however they chose to exist in those moments without his intervention.

Ellis grew up in Virginia Beach, then moved to New York to study music theory at Columbia University. A Fulbright fellowship later sent him to Brazil. He speaks fluent Portuguese, but his stutter was so intrusive during his nine months living in South America that many days he was left effectively mute. He worried that the Brazilians he met assumed he hadn't bothered to learn their language. Speaking plays a unique role in his family lineage: Ellis's grandfather, great-grandfather, and great-great-grandfather were all ministers, and his mother, an uncle, and a cousin are all stutterers.

"Within the evangelical tradition I was raised in, I felt that my stutter might be a demon, or the devil," he told me. Many weeks, at the end of the service, Ellis would walk to the altar and receive a prayer of healing to "cast out" his stutter. He no longer identifies as Christian but still prays every morning.

His stutter is a huge part of his work, though he still feels somewhat ambiguous about it in his daily life. "Sometimes I feel guilty for wasting somebody's time," he said. "I feel frustrated. I feel angry. I feel ashamed. I also feel very grateful, and very, like, blessed."

Ellis told me that, contrary to what he learned in church, stuttering has actually brought him closer to God. He believes that a long, painful block can be a door that leads to other feelings and truths. When a block starts to happen, his chest will become tight and he may temporarily stop breathing. For him, entering a long block is like putting himself in a prayer closet. Sometimes he feels like he's coming into contact with the divine, or with relatives he's never met.

"I kind of leave my body, and then I only come back once

the block is over," he said. "It's as if my mouth is the front door, and I leave through the back somewhere." He explained how he watches himself from above, searching for the sound in real time. He sees the listener waiting and wondering about what's happening as seconds tick by. He compares this sensation to being on the other side of a waterfall, standing between the heavy flow and the rock. It happens most frequently when Ellis tries to say his own name. "There's this feeling I often have that's like, in that time, I have no name, and I only get it back, or I only am baptized, once the block ends," he said. "But in the space of the block, there is, for me, an exceptionally profound freedom that arises."

Still, the momentary liberation doesn't fully compensate for the lifelong pain of stuttering. As a kid, Ellis gravitated toward friendships with girls, feeling more comfortable around them than he did with boys.

"I feel that, within Black communities, especially Black masculine spaces, there often is a quite intense policing of language—that if you don't speak in a certain way, if you don't use certain slang words or you don't speak with a certain cadence or a certain rhythm, a rhythm that is very influenced by rap, then you are not a part of the group," he said. "I couldn't speak. I could hear the cadence, and I could hear the vocabulary that was being used, but I couldn't match it, you know? It was like a song that I just couldn't play on my instrument. I felt excluded a lot of the time."

In the weeks before we first spoke, Ellis had developed a daily practice of studying runaway slave advertisements. Each morning for months, he would wake up and select a posting from an online archive. The more he did this, the more he began to notice symmetry.

"White owners would place an ad in the newspaper with a description of the enslaved person, what they were wearing, if they have any scars or characteristics, where they think they might be going, and a reward," Ellis said. "And there are hundreds of these that mentioned enslaved people who stutter, or who have speech impediments."

As he came across more of these postings, he noted all of the variations of the word "runaway." He began crafting lines using words found in the original advertisements. *The stutterer shall run away from any government / The stammerers ran five miles away from the speech.*

"Stuttering is hereditary, of course, as is my Blackness. My mother is who I got my stutter from. Presumably, the stuttering in my body comes from ancestors. I've been looking at these ads, and there's a number of them from Jamaica, which is where my mother is from. And when I look at those, there's this shiver that I get, which is that there is a small chance—but there's a chance—that one of them is an ancestor of mine, an enslaved person who stutters."

On New Year's Day at St. Mark's, Ellis closed his performance by quoting the civil rights advocate Kimberlé Crenshaw: *Treating different things the same can generate as much inequality as treating the same things differently.*

About a year and a half later, Ellis was scheduled for an outdoor performance at Lincoln Center, and we met for dinner in Brooklyn. He wore a black leather baseball hat and blue pants that glowed under streetlights as we walked. We ordered at the counter at Peaches HotHouse and we each struggled to say the names of our food. I stuttered on "chicken sandwich." He stuttered on "kale salad." I kept watching the woman behind the register to see how she would react. She was patient. She didn't give either of us The Look. When he's caught in a block, Ellis doesn't really jerk his head or move his hands like I do. Instead of looking down, he stares off into the distance. He holds his mouth open like a silent whistle, almost like he's wrapping his lips around an invisible saxophone. He eventually gets the word out and snaps back into conversation like nothing happened.

After dinner we went back to my apartment to listen to records. He pulled a Coleman Hawkins album off the shelf and we talked about the way musicians have to play and adapt to whatever room they're in—not unlike stutterers. He knocked on my door a few months later with a test pressing of his own vinyl record. We sat down on my couch and listened to it. He played every instrument on the album: saxophone, piano, synthesizer, drum machines. There was also a spoken-word component: He had turned one of the runaway slave advertisements into a song.

I've spent a lot of time thinking about the way JJJJJerome has chosen to spell his first name. He's experimented with different variations of it—from as many as fifteen "j's" down to the five that are there now. It's a beautiful word when you visualize it. All the little curves in the front look like a row of umbrella handles, but they lack their tops, their purpose. When you read "JJJJJerome" out loud, there's an inherent musicality to it. Depending on your preference, the juh-juh-juh-juh-juh can sound clean and rhythmic, much like the steady train of "b's" during "Bennie and the Jets." That song doesn't at all give you the sense that Elton John is making fun of people who stutter, but that he's using a stutter as a musical instrument. But you can also read the juh-juh-juh-juh-juh in a way that makes the "j's" jagged—like the way Roger Daltrey breaks time and turns on a wild stutter during the verses of the Who's "My Generation." When I read the word that way, I think back to Kenny in fifth grade, screaming "J-J-J-J-J-J-J-JOHNNNNN!" in the school cafeteria.

"The way I speak often leads to an antagonistic relationship with time," Ellis said. "When the stuttering is happening, there's kind of a veil. There's something happening that I don't fully understand, even though it's happening inside of me, and it's originating in me and spreading from me. And I find that very powerful, because I also feel this great deal of respect for it. I'm just like, 'You're—you just need—you're just doing your thing.' And I don't have control over it, I know I don't have full understanding of it, and that's okay. But it's taken me many years to arrive at that approach to it."

Pink Slips

My first layoff came four days before my twenty-sixth birthday. Digital First Media had convened a panel of newsroom leaders to introduce dramatic cost-saving measures across the company. Many of my colleagues had predicted the group would ultimately recommend putting one or more of the chain's newspapers up for sale. But they came up with an even more efficient idea: shut down the New York office and get rid of the fifty or so journalists who worked there. "Lofty Newspaper Project Is Closed After Two Years," said *The New York Times* that spring.

Just three years earlier, David Carr, the *Times* media columnist, had written a widely read profile of Digital First's CEO, John Paton. This paragraph near the end of the piece is telling:

Mr. Paton hears all sorts of clocks ticking. His newspapers are mostly owned by hedge funds and investment banks, which are not known for patience, and part of the reason that the percentage of digital revenue is rising so fast is that the print revenue that it is compared with is dropping so precipitously. Although he is something of an evangelist, he says he is also a pragmatist.

Paton used to sit behind an ornate wooden desk in the back corner of our open-floor-plan office. I worked about a dozen feet from him at one of the anonymous long white tables with lime-green dividers. I had been on the job for less than eighteen months when they handed us pink slips. It was a welcome kick in the ass: now I had no excuse not to find a new gig.

Job hunting is particularly challenging when you're a stutterer. You're constantly trying to prove your qualifications, and every time your speech breaks down during an interview, you lose confidence. Of course the hiring manager notices. It's a painful routine: Find a job posting and, if you're extremely lucky, email someone who *might* know someone who *might* vouch for you. Stutter like hell as you say your name at the security desk. Take a sweaty, blurry photo. Shove the guest pass in the breast pocket of your blazer, next to an old pass from a different building, reminding you of another job you didn't get. Stutter uncontrollably from start to finish during the interview, then send a slightly needy thank-you email to every person you met that day, dreading their pity but shamefully hoping for a pinch of it. If you didn't *totally* blow it, you'll be asked to write a memo with all your ideas for how to do the job. Spend about thirty hours crafting this ten-page document and read it approximately fifty-four times. Space out imagining yourself with your own desk and nameplate and business cards and slot on the masthead. Wait three weeks. Get no response. Fail to sleep. Write, then rewrite, then re-rewrite your cringeworthy "just checking in" email. Keep hearing nothing. Self-loathe. Check Twitter and notice that someone who seems smarter and wittier than you just announced they got the job you applied for.

That spring, during an interview at Condé Nast, I nearly passed out from blocking badly when speaking with HR. I watched the recruiter try to maintain a smile even though she seemed horrified. She thanked me for coming and said she would call upstairs to check in with the *Vanity Fair* editor I was supposed to meet next. I rode the elevator up and took a seat in the lobby. I sat there panicking for twenty minutes. When we shook hands, his first words indicated that the conversation was over before it started: "Well, I don't have much time . . ."

That same week I had an interview at *SPIN*. This was more my speed. The magazine shared a small, laid-back office with *VIBE* in a much better part of town. I took a seat in the editor in chief's office and we immediately hit it off, riffing about music and writing. He paid no attention to my stutter. We talked for over an hour, then he smiled and said he'd be back in touch very soon. He told me he had a good feeling about me. Four days later I opened my email and saw a new message from him. My heart raced. *This is it. This is the day my life changes.* He was writing to let me know that he had just been let go.

I had one more option that spring, and it seemed like a long shot. Six months earlier, I had applied for a digital role at *Esquire*. I made it to the memo stage but didn't get the job. Now they were shuffling some folks around and it sounded like there might be an opening. I was forty-five minutes early for my two p.m. interview with David Granger, the magazine's editor in chief. I sat on a stone ledge surrounding the Columbus Circle fountain just outside Central Park. I looked up at the sun and tried to steady my breathing. As I rode the escalator to the mezzanine of Hearst Tower, a surprising sense of calm washed over me. I fixed my hair in the back-mirrored wall of the elevator. For the first time in ages, I didn't look scared. I stepped off on the twenty-first floor and an executive assistant walked me past framed covers from the 1960s golden age—Muhammad Ali, Andy Warhol—to the conference room. Granger came in a few minutes later with a nonchalant stride. He looked like he had stepped out of the photo that accompanied his editor's letter each month. He was mellower than I'd imagined. He spoke in short, confident bursts and barely asked me any questions about journalism. We just talked about life. He told me to send him a memo about their iPad edition with my ideas, and, a few weeks later, he invited me back to meet with another editor. When I finally got the offer, I nearly fainted. It all seemed too good to be true.

GRANGER HAD HIRED ME to be an associate editor on *Esquire Weekly,* the smaller tablet spinoff of the monthly magazine. Remember, this was the 2010s, when glossy publications thought that digital bells and whistles, specifically made-for-iPad products, would save the publishing industry. It would take most of the decade for the people in power to realize that the only thing readers want to pay for is a high-quality story. I was responsible for a recurring mini-feature, "This Week in the Life of the American Man." My job was to gather nuggets from local newspapers and TV broadcasts around the country and weave them into a tapestry of feel-good stories for the opening section of each issue. Here's an old one I found:

June 5, 2014

LETTERS TRAVELED BY SEA

A Utah man, Clint Buffington, examined the sixtieth message in a bottle he'd discovered while on family trips to the Caribbean. He told a reporter that he's made contact with a quarter of the senders and personally met four of them.

A LIFE-SAVER VANISHED

In St. Augustine Beach, Florida, a man in his early twenties saw a woman about a hundred yards from shore at dusk, screaming for help. He swam to her, and returned her to safety. After catching his breath, with the woman safe, the man stood up and walked away before anyone could catch his name.

A CAFFEINE FIX WAS TRULY NEEDED

An ambulance technician in search of morning coffee happened to be wearing a carbon-monoxide detector when he entered a Dunkin' Donuts in Carle Place, New York. The detector went off—triggered by a gas leak coming from an oven vent—and potentially saving the employees' lives.

I did some light editing on other small stories each week and wrote occasional blog posts for the website, but that was basically it. I felt nervous about how *unbusy* I was in a given five-day period. Still, I showed up at the office early and stayed late every night. Granger was always on the floor before everyone. At dawn, he'd drive down from his home outside the city and read the *Times* in print on the leather couch in his office, high above Eighth Avenue. He would ingest the whole paper, plus another paper or two, as well as various feature story drafts, well before the morning production meeting. He'd walk around the office and say hello to every employee by name, looking you right in the eye. When I could sense him coming I'd rehearse my reply: *Hi . . . hey . . . hello.* "H" sounds were still tough for me. I eventually settled on "Morning!" with a quick nod.

On Monday, July 21, 2014, Granger walked up to my desk. He sat in the empty chair next to me and leaned forward with both elbows on his knees.

"So, I've got some bad news."

Hearst was shuttering *Esquire Weekly.* I was totally disoriented. I felt sick. He took me down to the fourteenth floor to meet with HR. Now the pattern was repeating itself, the emotionless benefits manager taking me through a corporate folder of "next steps." I was barely listening. I walked out of the building and into Central Park in disbelief. This was different than Digital First: *Esquire* had been my dream; now it was my nightmare.

I never got the full story of what happened. Nate, the other editor my age who worked on the *Weekly,* was shuffled into another role. I wondered why the same thing didn't happen to me, and, right or wrong, I blamed my stutter. Whenever I'd trudge through difficult phone interviews at my desk, I could swear that I was feeling the molecules in the room change, like the first day of ninth grade. *Maybe they didn't know it was this bad and used this as an excuse to get rid of me,* is the thought that echoed in my head all summer. Mike, *Esquire*'s digital director, assured me that it really was just a last-in, first-out scenario due to corporate budget bullshit. Granger, too, told me that my work had been "stellar." But I still felt like I was drowning and everyone was watching.

When I went back to work the next day, Granger called me into his office. He had a consolation prize: an offer to keep me on as a contract blogger for the website until I found a new full-time job. I'd have to register with a temp agency, and at some point the well would go dry, but it was something. I said thank you and kept showing up early and staying late for months. All my colleagues kept saying some version of "Sorry about what happened," and I'd smile and nod and try to change the subject. I started looking for other jobs, but I didn't want any other jobs. I wanted to work here, in this building, at this desk. Then, in October, there was more shuffling: a new top digital editor came in, and he rehired me to a full-time position. My taxes were a mess that year.

AROUND THIS TIME, Matt and I had been trying to mend our relationship, with uneven progress. We'd see each other on Thanksgiving and Christmas and random days throughout the year, but we hadn't reached the point of effortless casual conversation, and we never really spoke about anything on a deep level. To be fair, Matt had been putting more effort in than I was. I could sense the sincerity in his small gestures. He'd take me to baseball games whenever I was in D.C.; he'd never let me pick up the check or beer tab. In late January, he took the train up to New York to celebrate his thirty-first birthday. The weekend got off to a great start: he and Jennie both seemed genuinely proud and impressed when I gave them a tour of the *Esquire* office. I had been dating a great girl, Emily, who got us all a table at Lucien, a shoulder-to-shoulder French restaurant across the street from my old apartment in the East Village. After dinner we wandered west along Bleecker Street and met up with one of Matt's college friends and Jennie's brother before the final stop of the night: the Comedy Cellar.

A comedy club is a dangerous place for a stutterer, but I

had a strategy. Whenever a comedian would look in my general direction, I'd quickly stare down at my drink and try to make myself invisible. It always felt like playing with fire, but it worked. I had been to the Cellar a handful of times, as had Matt. But before that night, I had never shown up in a large group. A little before midnight all six of us descended the basement stairs, passing under the Cellar's glowing black-and-white sign. The hostess seated us at a large table with a dead-center view of the stage.

I squeezed in next to Emily. Matt and Jennie were a couple of seats away. The first few comedians came and went, some funnier than others. We smiled and laughed and kept ordering drinks. Then the host introduced the first name on the bill any of us recognized: Sherrod Small. He bounded up onstage and loosened the mic from the stand. He peered around the packed room. Then he pointed at me.

"Relationship guy!"

Oh god.

I looked over my shoulder, praying he was talking to someone else. He wasn't.

"What's your name?"

". . . .

". . . . .

". . . . .

". . . . ."

I panicked. I blocked hard. I couldn't say *anything.* I eventually blurted out, "I'm from here!"

He laughed and shot me a confused look. He hadn't asked where I was from. Now he had something to work with. He jokingly asked if I was afraid of him because he was Black.

"No, seriously, what's your name?" he said.

". . . . . j"

". . . . . juh"

I couldn't get it out.

". . . . . juh

". . . . . j"

He smiled. People in the audience were getting nervous.

". . . . . juh

". . . . . juh"

I jerked my head and fluttered my eyes. My neck veins were popping.

". . . . . juh

". . . . . juh . . . . juh . . . . juh . . .

". . . . . juh-j-uh-j-j-jOHN."

For a moment, the room was quiet. Small looked around at the crowd. His eyes narrowed like Sylvester the Cat. He let out a belly laugh.

"What do you do?" he asked.

". . . . . I'm . . . .

". . . . . I'm . . . .

". . . . . I'm . . . ."

People were cackling, cringing. Some were groaning.

". . . . . I-uh . . . . . I'm . . . ."

Matt swooped in and yelled the answer for me.

"He's a journalist!"

Out of the corner of my eye, I saw him and Jennie making the "cut it" motion at their necks. But that only made things worse. Small contorted his face and mocked the motion back at them. Now he was really fired up. He gave them the finger and yelled "Fuck you!" into the microphone. I was still blocking and twitching. I blinked rapidly with my head looking down at the table. Small laughed and shook his head. Then he moved on to someone else in the room.

It felt like an hour had passed. In reality, the whole thing probably lasted less than two minutes. I threw Emily a nervous smile and tried to slow down my heart rate. I wasn't embarrassed for myself so much as I felt bad for everyone else at the table. They looked like they had just witnessed a car accident. When the show ended, all six of us awkwardly pretended that nothing had transpired. We hugged good-bye outside the Cellar and Matt and Jennie made their way back to their hotel. Emily and I climbed into a cab and, the moment the door thunked closed, she began to sob. We crawled in traffic toward the Brooklyn Bridge in silence.

I felt a vibration in my pocket: a text from Matt. He told me he was sorry I had to go through all of that. He said it had taken every bone in his body not to charge the stage and strangle Small. I told him thanks, but that it was no big deal; we were in a dark room with a hundred people we'd never see again; this kind of stuff happens. I didn't want to talk about it. This was how I had learned to deal with moments like this growing up: Suppress it. Bury it deep down inside, in a place you'll never go. Summon an artificial smile. Move on. Jennie tweeted angrily at Small. The next morning, he tweeted back at her: "Eat a dick."

Emily and I are no longer together, but we've stayed in intermittent touch over the past several years. I recently asked her what she remembered about sitting next to me that night at the table.

"It was like a scene in a movie—it felt like there was a spotlight on you—I looked at Matt and Jennie, and they looked at me, and we all didn't know what to do," she said. "I felt really sad. And I felt so angry at the same time. Like, I wanted to punch that guy, because it felt like he was hurting you, you know? If I would have gotten called on, I would have felt so anxious speaking in front of people—heart racing, sweaty palms, all of that—so I could imagine you feeling that times a hundred."

Emily is among the most empathetic and caring people I've ever met. The night was so far behind us, but there was still pain in her voice as she described it.

"When we got home, I remember asking if you were okay, and you were like, 'Yeah, I'm fine.' And I don't know how long after, but your dad was in town. I don't know why, but I told him about it. Do you remember?" she asked.

My dad was in New York a week later for business. One night, I was out walking our dog, and he and Emily were chatting up in our apartment. When I opened the door and unhooked the leash, I knew something was wrong. My dad's face was sagging.

"I felt so bad that I told him, but I wanted to talk to someone about it," Emily said. "I'm sure he experienced things like that with you. But your dad was *so* upset, and I felt awful that I brought it up, because he probably was reminded of that pain, and the feeling that he couldn't protect you."

I can't blame Emily for wanting to talk about it with him. I wasn't emotionally capable of addressing my own pain, let alone hers as my partner. I was always trying to be tough. I didn't know what to do other than close myself off.

I've thought about that night at the Cellar a lot since it happened. Six years later, I contacted Sherrod Small. I had no idea if he would remember me. He asked where in the venue I was sitting that night. As I described the way I looked while I was violently blocking, the moment suddenly came back to him. What he said surprised me.

"I don't think anybody knew it was a stuttering thing," he said. "I think the audience probably got uncomfortable because they didn't know how I would handle it, or how our interaction would go. If I would have known, or if you would have told me, we would have had a great interaction together, because I've had other people in my life who stutter," he said.

Because I rarely stutter in the traditional sense—rapid repetitions—many people don't know what to make of my disfluency. I've had people ask me if I have Parkinson's, or epilepsy, or any number of other problems. It always feels impossible to look them in the eye and say, "No, I stutter."

Small never apologized to me. Was I expecting him to? Maybe. Then again, he wasn't pitying me.

"We could have easily just talked about it and it wouldn't have been like, a thing. You know?" he said. "I understand how people get uncomfortable with things like that, but the vibe between me and you would have then dictated the whole room."

Some people might call this night my stuttering horror story, but what right do I have to sit there and laugh as a comic mocks someone else's defining feature, then get upset when the spotlight shines on me? There are numerous stuttering comedians who have tried to make themselves the butt of the joke: Drew

Lynch, Nina G, and "Stuttering John" Melendez from *The Howard Stern Show,* to name a few. Why do we feel comfortable laughing at some things but not others?

I told Small that I don't necessarily look back on that night with a lot of *pain,* but that it was just so raw and overwhelming.

"An unanticipated naked moment—I definitely get that," he said. "But I think there's a lot of power in those moments. And the more we don't make it seem like it's a fucking *thing,* the more it becomes comfortable. Whenever you try to put it under the sheets or keep it a secret, that's when it can go awry."

What if I had actually just stood up and owned it? Small and I kept talking, and even traded a few laughs as the conversation went on. "I'm glad you reached out, I really am," he said.

I felt lighter afterward. But it made me wonder what else I hadn't addressed.

The Locked Box

I often think about an early therapy scene from *The Sopranos,* when Dr. Melfi prods Tony to talk about his anxiety and depression. Tony's eyes flare. He fumes. "Whatever happened to Gary Cooper?" he asks. "The strong, silent type. *That* was an American. He wasn't in touch with his feelings—he just did what he had to do."

Nobody wants to hear that they should go—or return—to therapy. Generations of us grew up in a culture that associated therapy with failure. We were led to believe that those who "need to talk to someone" are weak, that they don't have their shit together, that the normal thing to do is suck it up and deal with it like everyone else.

That's how I felt for decades. As a kid, I was forced to see a variety of speech therapists because I had an ugly problem that no one else in class had. I was different; normal people didn't go to the little room. I stopped working with Joe when I went away to college because eighteen felt too old for speech therapy. I never considered trying to find a new therapist at Penn State, or in Denver, or in New York. I was over it. To be sure, I was still stuttering every day, and while my disfluency was impossible to ignore, I was adept at compartmentalizing my shame. I'd suffer through a bad phone call or an awkward introduction at work, or I'd meet someone at a party who would laugh in my face, and I'd pretend to ignore the pain. I'd tell myself that I was tough, that my hide had been built up after a thousand of these indignities. I didn't know how to speak fluently, but I knew how to cope.

The truth is that these moments—like that night at the Comedy Cellar—didn't roll off my back so much as enter my consciousness and travel way down inside me. I shoved them all into a locked box in the pit of my stomach. With each passing year, the box got bigger, and heavier. It wasn't just shame in there, but unaddressed childhood trauma. So long as I never opened it, I'd be fine.

And then it flung open.

IN THE SPRING OF 2017 I flew to Austin, Texas, to cover South by Southwest for *Esquire*. I was sitting alone in a dark Alamo Drafthouse theater, scribbling notes about a documentary called *The Work*. In the film, the cameras take you inside Folsom State Prison for intensive group therapy sessions. Men convicted of crimes sit side by side with visitors from the outside who haven't been sentenced to jail but are dealing with buried issues that are inhibiting their lives. Over the course of four days, both the incarcerated people and the free men push one another to open up about their struggles. Many participants resist. Early on, several of the men judge, scoff, and pay lip service to the whole ordeal. But eventually the dam breaks for everyone. Some of the men go into a blind rage after particular comments from group members prick their suppressed pain. They punch and writhe. Their neck veins pop. One of the visitors, Brian, emits a guttural howl that sounds like the devil is flying out of his chest. But after these bouts of explosive anger and violence come tears. Some men nearly collapse in exhaustion, having finally let this suppressed pain out of their body. In Brian's case, his face transforms after punching and screaming and crying. It's an epic expulsion of emotion. It takes multiple incarcerated men to restrain him. When the outburst is over, Brian's eyes are lighter. He literally looks like a different person.

As I sat in the theater watching all of this unfold, I started sobbing. I wept for over an hour, drenching my sleeves and notebook. The person next to me timidly handed me a coarse white napkin. It was the transitive property of emotion: I was living vicariously through the people onscreen, opening my box like any other member of the group therapy circle. When the film was over, I felt worn out. Confused. Relieved. I had experienced catharsis before, but never like this. I knew I had to go to therapy myself. Not speech therapy—psychotherapy. But it took me over a year to find the courage to do it.

A FEW MONTHS AFTER Emily and I broke up, Andrew and I signed a lease on a railroad apartment in Greenpoint. Most nights we'd talk on our long IKEA couch eating takeout chicken over rice from God Bless USA Deli. Andrew is a good listener. He had been going to therapy himself for a few years and had nothing but positive things to say about his experience. Every now and then he'd drop a hint that maybe it was time for me to talk to his guy. I'd say something noncommittal like "Yeah, you're probably right," then quickly change the subject. I did this over and over again for months. Avoiding the problem seemed safer than dealing with it. Plus, despite my sobfest in Austin, I couldn't shake my immature and closed-minded attitude about the word "shrink." Could I really not handle this baggage on my own? Was I really that fucked up?

I had started dating someone new, Stina, who worked in a different department at Hearst. I soon found myself falling into the same patterns with her—behaviors that had negatively affected relationships all through my twenties. I'd treat something as innocuous as a pile of laundry on a chair as a personal attack: *You left it this way because you don't love and respect me.* I'd get anxious around visits with my family, losing sleep for days before we'd see each other. Sometimes I'd avoid communicating with my parents and brother altogether. Stina and I had been dating for a little over two years and were now approaching an inflection point. We were both thirty years old. We talked about marriage, but the longer we were together, the less it seemed like we should be. She was fiercely individual and wanted to go live in another country for a while; I had friends and a career in New York and couldn't imagine leaving.

No relationship is perfect is the phrase I kept hearing in my head. *Just suck it up and propose.* I gave myself a series of tasks—ask her mom for her blessing, buy the ring, pop the question—with dates for each milestone. Every deadline passed uneventfully. I had told myself that I would "get it all done" by the Fourth of July, but, as summer started, I shut down. I could barely talk to her. I was waking up every day feeling like I might explode. I quietly wondered if I was on the verge of a nervous breakdown.

On a Sunday afternoon in early June, Andrew and I met up to talk. I told him that I was feeling something I'd never felt before. It was different from the anxiety or depression I'd previously known. This new thing felt like I was in a speeding car with no control over the brake pedal. I didn't know when my discomfort would stop, when the knots in my stomach would untie. Over Gchat the next morning, Andrew sent me the name and number of a therapist his shrink had recommended. Andrew was in a bit of a rut, too, and had just quit his job. He was preparing to go backpacking in Asia and suddenly had cold feet.

> ANDREW: I have all my clothes laid out on my bed. I'm just staring at them.
> ANDREW: don't want to pack em
> ME: just set a deadline
> ME: your bag will be packed by 1pm
> ME: or whenever
> ME: deadlines help me with everything I feel anxious about
> ANDREW: perfect advice

I entered the therapist's number in my phone that morning, but it took me several hours to actually make the call. I ducked into an empty conference room. A scratchy voice with an old-school New York accent picked up. I could barely get a word out. He hung up on me after several seconds. *Maybe it's a sign,* I told myself. Then I was mad at myself for thinking that. When I got back to my desk I looked up his profile on the *Psychology Today* website.

SPECIALTIES:
Anxiety
Substance Use
Family Conflict

I started typing an email—a version of which I've sent hundreds of times:

Hi George,
    We spoke by phone but got cut off . . .

He wrote back the next day, but we wouldn't be able to meet for a few more weeks. When the day finally came, I nearly backed out at the last minute. I rode the subway to West Fourth Street and stepped out by the basketball courts along Sixth Avenue. George works out of an old prewar building with a heavy metal door and a loud *annnnnnk* buzzer. The elevator lumbered up six floors and opened into a modest waiting room with magazines and a white noise machine. He walked out of an interior hallway a few minutes later and led me back to his office. I removed my backpack and took a seat on a small leather couch. George sat in an armchair a few feet away. He has curly gray hair and glasses and speaks in a straightforward, down-to-earth manner.

"So what do you want to talk about?"

I had an immediate flashback to my first session with Joe. The two of them look and sound nothing alike, but here I was, back in the little room. I was fifteen when I first went to Joe. Another fifteen years had passed and I felt almost as lost as I did back then.

". . . I-I . . . uh . . . I need to figure . . . some things out."

George isn't a speech therapist, so, to start, I had to explain my stutter. He nodded as I gave him a heads-up as to the various manifestations of it: the pauses, the blocks, the loss of eye contact. And then I told him about all my recently missed deadlines. He didn't analyze or interject, he just let me talk. Our session lasted fifty minutes. When it was over, I realized I had probably spoken for at least forty of those minutes. I couldn't remember the last time I had talked that much. I'd never had a *desire* to talk that much. But now I could feel the locked box cracking open. We made an appointment for the following week. I grabbed a dollar slice of pizza before catching the train home. When I got back to our apartment, Stina asked how it went. It already felt like something had irrevocably changed.

SO MY WEEKLY RITUAL begins again, the one I've known since elementary school. I start to feel a little queasy in the hours leading up to each session. I keep my head down on my way to the appointment. But George's little room is the first one I've ever been to that feels like home. The furniture is lived-in. There's one small window that overlooks an air shaft. He has a bookshelf and little paintings and a framed photo of Bob Dylan. When you're in this little room, you can't hide. It's just you and your shrink and your problem(s). Not to mention that, now that you're an adult, you're paying to be here. Every minute you waste lying to yourself, or to the other person in the room, is just a waste of your own money.

George reminds me of Robin Williams's character in *Good Will Hunting*. He doesn't use psychoanalytic terms or take notes on a legal pad. He's never in a rush. He just sits there and lets me go on and validates my feelings with small phrases. After a few weeks of sessions, I realize that I've basically been asking him for permission to end my relationship with Stina. But that just means I'm asking myself for permission. I tell him that sometimes I don't feel worthy of love. When I think ahead to marriage, or being a dad, or that part of life where you look like an older, grayer version of yourself, with wrinkles around the eyes and hairier forearms, I'm afraid I'll be alone. I've always been afraid of being alone. I think that's why I've clung to relationships even when they haven't made sense.

One Sunday in July, Stina and I drive to Jacob Riis Park for a day at the beach. We bicker the whole way there and don't talk much during the day. As she pulls out of the parking lot to come home, a car nearly T-bones us. She slams on the brakes and our seat belts tighten. We're in a tiny Smartcar—the collision could have killed both of us. I slam my hand against the roof of the car in frustration.

"JESUS CHRIST!"

She pounds the steering wheel and cries.

And then it tumbles out.

"Maybe I should move out," I say.

"Yeah, I think you should."

We sit in silence the whole way home. We're quiet all night, and the next day, and the day after. When Wednesday comes I tell George. He nods. I begin looking at apartment listings. A few weeks later I sign a lease.

My new living room sits above a falafel shop that blasts music through the floorboards every night. I become a regular at the pho place around the corner. There's an L-shaped counter filled with other seemingly single people scrolling their phones, staring into their rice noodles. I block and twitch trying to say my name to my new neighbors while jiggling my new key in my new door. Here comes the strained, huffing-and-puffing phone call to the credit card company, trying to confirm my new address.

After several sessions talking about the adjustment to single life, George and I start unpacking my family issues. This is stuff I've never talked about. It's a weird exercise to sit in a little room and articulate the ways you think your mom and dad and brother let you down. I feel guilty talking to him about it. I feel guilty writing about it right now. When I got my new place, my parents drove up to Brooklyn with an old air conditioner that my dad helped me wedge into the bedroom window. We sat on the living room floor late on a Sunday night, putting together an IKEA bookcase, pounding little pegs, cursing. My mom brought food and placemats and cloth napkins and all those other items I would have kept shoving to the bottom of my to-do list. How do you experience all of that and then turn around a few days later and tell your shrink that they still don't get it? That they never got it? I felt like a dick. But George didn't bat an eye. He wanted me to keep opening the box, especially when it came to my brother.

What did he do?

And why did your parents let him do it?

I HAD RECENTLY STARTED a new job at *Rolling Stone,* and I was scheduled to go to D.C. for several days for a work trip. I knew I had to see my brother. My nephew was now two and a half, and I barely knew him. I initially made plans to come to Matt's house for a family dinner. Then I sent a separate email.

October 8, 2018

Hi Matt,

 Looking fwd to seeing you on Wednesday night. I'd also like to have some one-on-one time to talk next week. Can you meet me for lunch or an early drink on Tuesday?

 John

Matt wrote back half an hour later.

Hi John, looking forward to your visit as well. The early drink sounds good Tuesday. I'll need to head home as

*of 5:30, and will be in gym clothes, but maybe 4:30 at
Stoney's? 21st and L, casual, awesome grilled cheese if
you choose to hang out after I leave and have a bite.*

He sent a follow-up email less than an hour after that:

Hi again John,

*I wish I was mentally tougher but to be honest and
from experience these sort of cryptic summits distract me
and put a dent in my mojo during the waiting period,
which in this case is 8 days long. Would you do me the
favor of a heads up of what you'd like to discuss, or, just
give me a call sometime sooner? I'd love to get together
Tuesday, just don't want to spend 8 days guessing/
worrying about it, ya know?*

Thanks, Matt

So this was my chance. No more avoidance. Matt and I
would sit down for a man-to-man conversation. I was terrified, but I was ready.

George and I had spent the previous few months processing
many hard memories, the stuff my family had tried to ignore.
I told him that I eventually wanted to put it all on the table
with Matt but that I was afraid of what he would do as I began
to speak. As the date of my D.C. trip got closer, George and I
started practicing the conversation in his office. Sometimes I'd
get lost in a monologue and his face would blur and it'd feel
like I was really talking to my brother.

I continued rehearsing what I wanted to say over and over
on the Amtrak to Washington. Pulling into Union Station always
felt like entering a time warp, like I was going to walk past my

younger self gazing at the huge holiday train set in the atrium. I showed up early at the empty sports bar and grabbed a two-top. Matt walked in a few minutes later and looked older than I remembered. We exchanged a clunky handshake-hug-hello. We mumbled through a few minutes of painful small talk and forced smiles. *This place is great. Things are great. Work's great.*

"So what do you want to talk about?" he asked.

I stuttered through my first sentence. I told him that I had started going to therapy to try to work through some of the stuff from our past.

"Good for you," he said. He gulped his beer and looked away.

"Do you remember what it was like?" I asked.

Matt blew up as I began recalling specific memories from our childhood. I acted out the way he used to mock my most intense moments of disfluency—straining my neck, emitting a dull whine, pressing a palm against my forehead to force out the missing word. He accused me of lying. It felt like he was attempting to keep me from talking.

"What are you even trying to prove here?" he barked. There was an unfamiliar fear in his eyes.

I told him that I felt like there was a locked box deep inside me. "There's one inside you, too," I said. "And I'm in there."

For the first time, I told him about the stuttering shame I carry around every day. He didn't really have an answer. He nearly stormed out multiple times, but he ultimately stayed and listened. After four hours of conversation, I said something that seemed to penetrate his shell. I asked how he would react if someone started tormenting his son. I asked what he would do if, god forbid, his kid had a disability and this person made him feel small because of it. He steamed—not at me, but at this hypothetical. He looked like he wanted to murder this nonexistent person. He rubbed his palm against the back of his neck. He looked worn out.

I was exhausted, too, but I felt like I was beginning to let go of something. I told him that we didn't have to dwell on our childhood every day for the rest of our lives, but that I needed to just say this stuff out loud—that I needed him to acknowledge its existence. This was something I had come to realize with George: my pain wasn't taking up so much space because I kept reliving trauma, but because it felt like my family wanted to act like none of it had even happened. All the polite smiles and various other forms of self-preservation had invalidated my experience. *That's* what hurt. That's what I wanted—needed—to change. But was it too much to ask of someone else? Was he ready to do that? Were my parents ready?

We eventually stood and hugged and paid the tab. Neither of us had eaten dinner. He went home to his family many hours after he was supposed to. I went to a dive bar and ate a burger and fries, staring at the wall. It was a strange night. It felt like I had shaken up the snow globe that was our relationship and all the little snowflakes were still trying to settle to the bottom. I began to think they wouldn't for a long time.

I showed up at Matt's house for dinner the next night. I gave him and Jennie a big hug and sat next to my nephew on the couch. Matt and I both tried to act normal, but things were different. He seemed to be tiptoeing around me in an unfamiliar way. When I left, we hugged again. The power dynamic had shifted. I didn't know what to feel.

20

"Our Bodies Betray Us"

It was six days before Christmas, two months after my conversation with Matt. I had come back to New York after that experience feeling like a stronger person. I told my brother that I didn't want this one hard, long conversation to be a fleeting moment, but for it to open up a new dialogue between us—for us to start building something new. But I don't know how clearly I actually expressed that idea when we parted ways.

Still, I felt better than I had in a decade. The box inside me was now more open than it had ever been, and while it wasn't empty, it didn't feel as heavy. I was ready to fully give myself to someone in a way I hadn't since Sam in college or Julie in sixth grade. I had been in and out of relationships through my twenties and had never before used a dating app. So I decided to give it a try. I was immediately way in over my head. I sat in my apartment, scrolling through old photos on my phone, trying to find half a dozen or so that looked presentable. Those endless taps through your personal archive can fuck up your brain—all those people and places you may have tricked yourself into forgetting.

I eventually landed on a picture from a trip to Los Angeles. In the image, I'm standing in front of a black, white, and red swirling mural—the cover of Elliott Smith's *Figure 8,* one of my favorite albums from high school. As I posed, I could picture him standing there with one hand in his pocket, looking off to the left all cool and unbothered. I stood in front of the wall and smiled like a dork.

On Monday morning of the last work week before the holidays, I stepped off the train at Forty-Seventh Street with my head down, looking at my phone. I came up the stairs and out onto Sixth Avenue under the glowing Radio City Music Hall marquee. Throngs of tourists were already lined up to see the Rockettes at that morning's *Christmas Spectacular* performance. I opened the app. Swipe. Swipe. Swipe. A new profile popped up: a short girl with brown hair in all black, standing in front of the exact same mural from my photo. I nearly dropped my phone on the sidewalk. Her name was Liz. I messaged her.

I like your photo.

It was barely nine thirty on a Monday morning. What am I doing? What kind of desperate psycho is swiping at this hour? She wrote back a few hours later.

I like yours.

We spent the whole day messaging about music. She had impeccable taste. I asked if she was free for a drink that week.

Have you ever been to Sharlene's?
That's my favorite bar.

The next two days were torturous. I kept glancing down at my phone to check the time. When the night came, I texted her as I was leaving work.

Heading to train now. That's my mission control status.

Where the hell did this come from? It didn't even sound like me. I saw the three little dots that meant she was typing back.

Ground control to Major John. Thanks for the status update.

I smiled, remembering how much she loved David Bowie. I got down to the platform just as the train was pulling in. I texted back before losing service.

Rest assured I have taken my protein pills.

She didn't miss a beat.

Check fare ticket and may subway gods be with you.

Forty-five minutes later Liz and I are sitting at the end of the bar. It's dark and humming. That spilled beer scent wafts across the room. I decide to do something I've never done with a girl: I open up about my stutter within the first fifteen minutes of conversation. I have no idea why I'm compelled to do this. Something tells me I don't have to hide it. She sips her tequila soda. Her face is totally neutral. She nods. "I have this thing," she says.

She's a full foot shorter than I am. When she turns to the side and moves her hair I can see a long scar across the top of her skull. She starts telling me about her thing, dystonia, a neuromuscular disorder.

"We seem to have a lot in common," I say.

Liz smiles. "Because our bodies betray us?" she asks.

She tells me that her thing started small: problems in her hands that made it hard to hold a pen and write her name. As a teenager the trouble spread to her legs and feet. In the middle of college, her legs would violently contort and spasm at all hours of the day, making it impossible to walk. She eventually took a leave of absence from school to have brain surgery. Doctors implanted two electrodes on both sides of her frontal lobe and ran electrical wires down through her neck to a pacemaker-like object in her chest. The treatment is known as deep brain stimulation, or DBS for short. When the device is programmed and running properly, her muscles can function more or less like anyone else's. But when it's not, her body starts to betray her again. The battery inside her dies about every two years and has to be replaced. She tells me all of this nonchalantly, without a hint of embarrassment, shame, or discomfort. I'm just sitting there, trying to take it all in. Liz sips her drink and smiles.

"I'm part robot," she says.

Even though she seems at peace with it in the moment, she explains how that wasn't always the case. She experienced it all: the judgment, the pity, the self-loathing, the isolation. I'm mesmerized as she speaks. She smiles and touches my hand. How did we find each other? Neither of us had included these particular aspects of our lives on our dating profiles.

I grab a pair of coasters to put over our drinks. We walk toward the back of the bar, where the jukebox hangs on the wall catty-corner to the pinball machines. Liz reaches into her wallet and fetches a pile of dollar bills. I lean one arm on the glass and we start picking songs. All of her selections are flaw-less. She turns to go to the bathroom off a little hallway bathed in harsh white-yellow light. Then her next pick starts playing:

Pavement's "Gold Soundz." It's one of my favorite songs of all time with one of my favorite lyrics of all time: "You can never quarantine the past."

Now it's getting late. I ask Liz if she wants to have one more drink and she says yes. We keep hanging out that night, and the next night, and the next night. We don't even go out; we just drink red wine and listen to records and watch *A Charlie Brown Christmas.* But then it's suddenly almost Christmas Eve. I take the train down to Philly and she flies home to L.A. We never stop texting. On New Year's Eve we meet back in New York and I introduce her to three of my closest friends, Ryan, Matt, and Caprice. It's only me and Liz's fourth night together, but it feels like our thousandth.

LESS THAN FOUR MONTHS later we're on a plane to California. Liz wants me to join her family for Passover. We decide to take a few extra days and fly into the Bay Area, then rent a car and drive down the Pacific Coast Highway. It's mid-April, so it's still chilly, but the sky is blue and the roads are empty. I've wanted to do this drive ever since reading Jack Kerouac as a college sophomore. We're blasting George Harrison's *All Things Must Pass* with the windows down. The two-lane highway snakes along foothills while waves crash into the craggy rocks below us. Her hair is billowing in the breeze.

We come around a bend and cross Bixby Bridge and check into Big Sur Lodge. The next morning we wake up with the sun and walk among towering redwoods, taking huge breaths of that hyperoxygenated air. We drive down to Pfeiffer Beach and feel the cold spray of the ocean water against our faces. The Pacific changes colors up close: sometimes it looks teal, sometimes baby blue, sometimes a deep, dark navy. The sand has a trippy purple tint. We ask a stranger to take our photo in front of a huge rock jutting out of the surf. I put my arm around Liz's waist and grip her puffer jacket. From a distance I look happy. Zoom in and I look preoccupied.

As we start getting closer to Liz's house, I feel a pit in my stomach. I've never been to a Passover seder. There will be fifteen of us sitting around her parents' dining room table. Over a two-hour period, we will take turns reading the story of Passover out loud. I haven't read anything out loud in this round-robin fashion since high school.

I'm thinking back to Latin class. I can still hear the bellowing laugh. We're trudging through passages about ancient Rome, one by one, up and down the rows. My cheeks feel like they're a thousand degrees. My vision blurs as my head hangs down over the textbook. I'm trying to push out the first word. No sound. Now I'm forgetting to breathe. The asshole in the corner is cackling.

On the last morning of our trip, we wake up in Solvang and eat breakfast at the counter of Paula's Pancake House. Liz can sense my building anxiety. She puts her hand on my knee. Now we're only a couple of hours away from her house. We drive down through Santa Barbara, past Zuma Beach, curve through Malibu. Surfers in camper vans form a ribbon along the coast. Palm trees start ticking by like skyscrapers.

Now I'm thinking back to middle school, during the really bad Matt nights, when I used to close my bedroom door and fantasize about packing up and leaving. I wanted to come here, to this long stretch of sand on the southern coast of California. I wanted to stare at the Pacific with my back turned to literally everything. I wanted to flee my family, my past, my anxiety, all the shame and pain of my stutter. And now I'm finally here, but so is my problem. I'm terrified of making an awful first impression on my new girlfriend's family. Liz has told me countless times that I can skip reading out loud altogether. It would be so much easier, and I want to do it. But if she is truly the one, and if we'll be back here at this same table next year, and the year after that, then what? What if we start our own family and Liz wants to continue this Passover tradition? Am I just going to cower in perpetuity?

The long dinner table is beautifully set. Liz's mom has gone above and beyond, leaving little printed names at each place setting. All the men, including me, are wearing white and blue yarmulkes. A bound copy of the family Haggadah, the Passover text, is waiting next to each plate. The reading starts counterclockwise, meaning I'll be the second to last person to go. Now I'm counting paragraphs, just like in middle school, trying to figure out which chunk of text I'll have to maneuver through. My heart speeds up and I start bouncing my right foot under the table. Nothing can calm my nerves at this point. Liz's parents are at opposite ends of the table. Her two older brothers are here, as is her sister, plus some cousins and family friends. I can barely remember anyone's name. Now I'm two readers away. I keep my head down, trying not to look anyone in the eye. The second I look up at Liz she's staring back at me with a sweet and soulful smile. She grabs my hand and squeezes it. Everyone turns to the next page in their book. Liz's younger sister is sitting to my left. She finishes her last sentence. Now it's my turn.

I've already read this paragraph half a dozen times in my head, but that doesn't matter. I start to recite the words out loud and immediately struggle. But I keep pushing through the sentences. My voice is shaky and uneven, as are my breaths, but everyone is patient. Nobody is interjecting, trying to take over the text and finish it for me. Everyone just sits and listens. I make it to the end of the paragraph and exhale. Liz starts reading the next one. I try to slow down my pulse and hope my cheeks are coming back to a normal color. And then the Haggadah starts its second lap. Then its third, its fourth, its fifth. With each reading, my fluency never improves, but I try to just let myself stutter. Eventually the word ends, and the sentence ends, and the paragraph ends. Soon someone else is reading. In time, we're eating brisket and laughing and singing songs as a big group. When it's over we all take a long neighborhood walk. Liz tells me she's so proud of me. About six months later, we move in together.

The Biden Letters

I'm sitting across from America's best hope to defeat Donald Trump. At times he appears to have difficulty maintaining eye contact. He blinks rapidly and wiggles his lips when he struggles with certain words. Joe Biden spent years telling a bootstraps story about "beating" his childhood stutter. But what if reality was more complicated than that?

I was four months into a new job at *The Atlantic* and still trying to get over debilitating imposter syndrome. I had been reading the magazine for years and long dreamed of working there, but I still felt like I wasn't operating at everyone's level. One of my old colleagues from Digital First Media, Adrienne, had been an editor there for a while and had always casually brought up the prospect of us working together again someday. Once or twice a year we'd meet for a drink and talk about story ideas, but a full-time job always seemed out of reach. Then all of a sudden I was there. I couldn't believe it.

In my first two weeks on the job, I had a series of introductory coffees and lunches with other editors and writers, during which I tried and failed to downplay the severity of my stutter. Denise, who oversees features, asked if I had any evergreen story ideas tied to the election. "Evergreen" is journalism jargon for articles that aren't explicitly newsy and, ideally, are pieces that will have a long shelf life. This is especially important for monthly print mags, for which stories may be assigned six months before an issue appears on newsstands. I told her that I had long thought about writing something about Joe Biden's life as a stutterer. She sat up a little in her desk chair.

"I never knew Biden had a stutter," she said.

This was May 1, 2019. Biden had entered the Democratic primary race a week earlier. On *The Daily Show,* Trevor Noah had already devoted a segment to Biden's verbal stumbles during his first rally—a slapstick supercut of repetitions and secondary behaviors, not unlike one that Fox News would broadcast later that summer. I told Denise that I could pick up on all the little things Biden was doing to try to keep his lingering stutter at bay—his blinks, his word substitutions, his head and hand movements. She seemed both fascinated and skeptical. After conferring with others, she encouraged me to pursue it.

I had never written anything directly about stuttering for public consumption. I didn't feel ready. So I stalled. It took me almost two months to email Biden's people to request an interview and nearly another two months for them to agree to let me talk to him.

On the last Tuesday of August, I showed up at his D.C. campaign office impossibly early and took a seat on the low brick wall outside. I opened my folder of questions and started practicing. After stuttering at the security desk I rode the elevator upstairs. Biden had just taken the Amtrak from his home in Wilmington, Delaware. An aide led me back to a small office. A blue-striped tie was slung over a hanger behind the desk chair. The TV on the wall was on mute, tuned to MSNBC. Biden stood up and we shook hands and he gave me a look as if we had met before. He rested his cell phone facedown on the desk between us. I had two recorders rolling that day, one aimed directly at him, one positioned between the two of us to pick up my voice.

Now it was happening again: I could barely ask a question without blocking on every word. Biden started telling me about his uncle who was a severe stutterer, then talked a lot about his mom.

"Constant reinforcement. Constant, constant, constant, constant reinforcement from my, my-muh-muh-mom and my dad," he said, unintentionally stuttering on the "m" sound. He had trouble with "r" a moment later. "My mom would say, 'Joey, rrrrr-emember, bravery rrr-resides in every heart. Every heart. And someday it will be summoned. And Joey, the courage you are demonstrating, standing up and taking this on, will serve you well your whole life, Joey.'"

Biden's pupils went wide as he described his mother. At times, he almost seemed to be channeling her, speaking to me as his younger self.

"She'd say, 'Joey, look at me, look at me!'"

He leaned in and pointed his finger.

"'Remember! Remember!'" His voice was suddenly sharp and punchy. "'You're smarter than anybody. No one's better than you—you're no better than anybody else—but no one's better than you, Joey. This does not define you. It's not who you are.'" He kept talking faster. "'Focus on the things you do well, Joey! You're a great athlete! You're really a bright young man! You're a nice-looking young man! You're a polite young man! *Remember!*'"

We talked for over an hour, but he seemed to be keeping some things close to the chest. That night, on the Amtrak back to New York, I listened to the recording of our interview and went over my notes. This was scribbled at the top:

Biden won't really admit he still stutters. What does that mean?

A week and a half later, I was following Biden on the campaign trail. In Laconia, New Hampshire, roughly two hundred people waited in line before his town hall inside the Belknap Mill, an old textile factory just off Main Street. Attendees climbed three flights of creaky stairs to get to the room where his aides had prepared a town hall. There was a small PA system and a taut American flag hanging behind the lectern. One of the warm-up speakers that day was John Burns, a twenty-three-year-old field organizer on Biden's New Hampshire team. I was standing in the back of the room reading an email on my phone when I heard it and suddenly looked up: Burns was blocking on the "j" in "Joe." *Hard.*

"It was in . . . fifth grade . . . that my speech . . . language pa . . . thologist . . . told me about a United States senator who . . . used to stutter just like me," Burns told the room. His breathing patterns were uneven. He swayed behind the lectern, occasionally closing his eyes and jerking his head. Biden acknowledged him at the beginning of his own speech. "And I want to thank, uh, uh, John Burns, our organizer," Biden said. "John is a, uh, you know, it takes a lot of courage for someone who has a stutter to stand up before a large group of people. And it takes an enormous courage to do it, uh, um, at a time when, uh, when we have, uh, folks, uh, in the media and, not in the media, in the White House that, uh, think it's okay to make fun of people. Um, and, uh, and, uh, so I want to thank you, John, and, uh, it takes uh, I said, a lot of courage, and you've done a great job."

As people filtered out, I leaned against a table in the back corner and waited for Burns. I complimented him on his ability to power through his speech. He said he'd practiced his introduction several times with coworkers and while driving alone, where he said he speaks "crazy fluent." He swayed as he talked and crossed his arms behind his back. He pinched his eyes closed on just about every stutter. And yet, he seemed happy and at peace. "You play out the worst-case scenarios in your head," Burns said. "But what I do a lot with public speaking, and it helped—I learned this in speech therapy: it's important to identify yourself as a person who stutters."

As weeks went by and I continued working on the story, my fluency plummeted. I couldn't sleep. I could barely eat. My hair started falling out. I spoke to scores of people from Biden's past, and, night after night, I'd sit hunched over my desk, listening to myself stutter horribly through interviews on the recorder. *Is this really what I sound like?*

Every story has that one interview that comes in late and ties it all together. For me, it was Michael Sheehan, Biden's debate coach and a fellow person who stutters. Sheehan spoke about the "two gifts" that a stutter gives you. He told me that he and Biden have had this conversation, too.

"The one good thing it gives you is just immense empathy," he said. "Because you know what it's like to be picked on, you know what it's like to be ostracized, you know what it's like to have people presume bad things about you, even though they don't know anything about you. You never want that to be visited on anyone else. And I think that's a wonderful gift that you never lose."

He paused.

"The bad gift it gives you—and I'm only going to presume that this is true about you, too, John—is it does give you an anger that is very deep. And I think it's an anger that comes out of frustration. It's an anger that comes out of you being excluded, or bad things have been thought about you with no justification whatsoever."

I wrote six drafts of the story. Most nights I'd come into the bedroom with my new pages and collapse beside Liz at one or two in the morning. I'd close my eyes and clasp my hands over my chest while she read each new draft to me aloud. We did this over and over for weeks. Some nights ended in tears for both of us.

At the end of October, I was nearing my deadline, and Liz needed another battery-replacement surgery. She dreads each trip to the hospital, but she never seeks pity from anyone. On the morning of that particular surgery, I was sitting in the waiting room at Cedars-Sinai in Los Angeles with her parents. Dystonia is a genetic disorder—Liz's mom has it, as did her grandfather. Her mom told me about how her dad tried to hide it, how he never wanted to acknowledge it was a problem as an old man. I told her he sounded a lot like Biden.

When my Biden article was finally published online just before Thanksgiving, I had no idea what to expect. At a minimum, I thought the stress of the assignment would finally recede. The piece immediately went viral. That afternoon, I received an email asking me to go on MSNBC the following morning to discuss it.

SO HERE I AM in the little room. It's just after eight a.m. I'm staring at the floor, waiting for them to call me in. My knee is bouncing. I didn't really sleep last night. A black car showed up outside my apartment this morning. I climbed into the backseat and chugged the little bottle of water waiting in the armrest. My stomach rumbled as the car zipped across the Manhattan

Bridge and up the FDR Drive into Midtown. I stepped out and took a picture of the glowing Rainbow Room marquee, then walked into 30 Rock. A production aide was waiting for me in the lobby. Soon I was upstairs in the makeup chair. Jeff, my boss, had been a guest on an earlier show that morning, so he swung by to wish me luck. He stood next to my chair wiping off his own pancake makeup with a tissue. We caught each other's eye in the long horizontal mirror. He turned around. "You know you don't have to do this," he said. I don't know exactly what I said back, but it was something about not wanting to hide anymore. It was a lie: a large part of me wanted to keep hiding.

A little while later I take my seat on set as the nine a.m. host, Stephanie Ruhle, reviews her script. Aides fuss with her hair and dust lint off her green dress. I'm wide-eyed and silent. I can hear a producer's voice in my right ear asking me to test the mic clipped to my blazer. The Atlantic's saintly PR team negotiated a "pre-tape" with MSNBC. In about half an hour, Stephanie will go live on air and start the top of her show, then at some point after a commercial break they'll insert this segment. We're doing it this way instead of truly live, because nobody—especially me—knows how bad it will be, if I'll be able to get a single sound out. I've never in my life considered the prospect of going on TV, let alone a fast-talking cable news show. TV people know how to modulate their voices and speak in shareable sound bites. They sit up straight, they project, they emphasize their point with their hands. You don't see stutterers on TV. If anything, the people you see on TV have spent years honing their skills to specifically *not* stutter on air. I wonder how high my pulse is. Now we're about to start.

The lights are insanely bright.

Okay, we're rolling.

Stephanie begins her introductory monologue:

"Former vice president Joe Biden came into the 2020 primary as an automatic front-runner. But after a series of disappointing debate performances, he is slipping in the polls and struggling to stay ahead of the pack. Gaffes aside, there is a key part of Biden's past that could explain those onstage missteps. A new story in *The Atlantic,* that I highly recommend, explores Biden's stutter, and how the former vice president still handles that challenge, specifically as he faces opponents in the Democratic primary. Joining me now, the author of that piece, John Hendrickson, senior politics editor for *The Atlantic.*"

The camera cuts to me.

I grip the clear desk.

I force a smile.

I swivel in the black chair.

"John, I'm so glad you're here. This story is very personal to you."

I nod. I gulp. I keep forcing smiles.

I'm trying to look at Stephanie and not at the large camera over her shoulder. I'm trying to speak slowly and avoid filler words. My speech is jagged and halting. I jerk my head up and down. I swallow. But I just keep talking. When she begins a new question, my shoulders rise and fall as I struggle to catch my breath.

About midway through the interview, she asks if people should be concerned about Biden facing off against Donald Trump on the debate stage, specifically if he has to deal with Trump's belittlement and verbal attacks.

"The president employs bully tactics," she says. "Bully tactics facing off against a stutter. What does that do?"

I'm not prepared for this question. I'm supposed to remain

politically neutral, especially in public. I have no idea what I'm going to say. I shake my head, then begin to speak.

"It makes you feel . . . shame. It makes you . . . wanna just . . . walk away. You know, even . . . coming on . . . your show this morning—I've never done TV before, this is . . . my . . . nightmare in a lot of ways. But . . . you know . . . the way to . . . overcome that . . . is to . . . talk about it. And it doesn't have to . . . be a . . . weakness. It can just . . . be a . . . part of you. This . . . thing that just exists."

WHEN I GOT HOME that night, I felt my shoulders fall for the first time in months. Liz collapsed in my arms, crying with pride. I let myself cry, too. We lay on the bed for nearly an hour, sobbing and laughing. The response to the story was like nothing I could have ever imagined. Emails from stutterers were pouring in from around the world. The next morning I went on NPR. More stutterers continued to contact me. The notes kept coming for days, then weeks, then months. These weren't dashed-off emails; they were personal, soulful, confessional missives.

There was Anu Hundeyin from Nigeria, who told me how she used to have to stomp around her house to get her words out. There was Niko Pittore from Texas, who had a stroke in utero, with the umbilical cord wrapped around his neck, cutting off oxygen to his brain, which doctors believe caused his stutter. There was Joe Zingsheim from Milwaukee, who at the age of seventy-seven went on a week-long psychedelic retreat in Mexico and took psilocybin mushrooms, hoping to rewire his stuttering brain. Holly MacDonald from British Columbia told me how her father could never accept her brother's disfluency, how he wouldn't allow the family to start dinner until her brother could answer a practice phone call without stuttering.

I couldn't believe so many strangers were opening up to me. Some people wrote multiple notes. I replied to every single person, and in many instances, like with Jim McKay, we struck up a regular correspondence that continues to this day.

Here's another email that changed my life:

> My name is Hunter Martinez. I am 32 and an attorney in Denver. I am married and have a newborn daughter. I grew up mainly in Fort Worth, Texas and have been stuttering for as long as I can remember. Several men in my father's family have very slight stutters, but nothing as bad as mine. My mother has battled mental illness for a long time, and when I was young she was taken to a mental hospital for a long period of time. This happened suddenly, and my father was a new physician. As a result, I was shuttled from friend's house to friend's house until my father could get time off of work to take care of me. I really do not remember this, but apparently I refused to eat during this period. The doctors said it was because it was the one thing I could control. I started eating again, but my stutter developed soon after.
>
> I refused to go to speech therapy for many years. I went to college at the University of Denver where I did not know a single soul. I eventually went to law school at DU. Law school is not the friendliest place to a stutterer, but with many patient and helpful peers and professors I was able to make it through, especially after an encouraging phone call from then Vice President Joe

Biden during my 2L year. It was a struggle to find a job after law school. None of the firms would admit it, but a mentor did tell me honestly that some people did not want to hire me because of my stutter. I was fortunate to finally get my chance and am now a senior associate at a firm in downtown Denver.

However, I must admit there are areas in which my fear of stuttering has held me back. As you probably noticed, I have a Latino last name. My father is Latino and Spanish is his first language. My mother is Caucasian, but was a Spanish teacher. However, I hated Spanish classes in school because I stuttered even worse when trying to speak Spanish. I was so frustrated that I gave up speaking Spanish my sophomore year of high school. Not knowing Spanish is one of my biggest regrets, but I am trying to learn now through an app on my phone. I hope that my daughter can learn Spanish and have the connection to her Latina heritage that I feel is missing because I do not speak Spanish.

I am sorry for the lengthy email. I had planned to just write you a couple of short paragraphs about myself, but just kept writing. Let me know if you would like to talk further about stuttering. We can correspond via email or, as Joe Biden called it, the hell beast invention known as the telephone. I have never really connected with a fellow stutterer and would enjoy doing so.

All the best,

Hunter

Hunter and I did start talking. Sometimes we would go back and forth in hour-plus sessions, trading laughs and various stutter horror stories. Sometimes we'd just fire off short emails with little life updates. Most of the time I'd hardly notice his stutter at all, but every now and then it would come out in full force.

A big guy with broad shoulders, Hunter told me that, as a young stutterer growing up, he intentionally tried to make himself appear smaller during moments of disfluency—a subconscious wish that others wouldn't see him struggle. That first time we spoke, I asked him to describe the moment a new stutter arrives. "It just gets, you know, it's like a blanket that's thrown over you," he said. "I have to think to breathe."

Around the holidays, he told me about revisiting home movies from distant Christmas mornings, back when he was four or five years old. He sat there and watched his younger self open presents under a glimmering tree at his childhood home. The little boy in the video stuttered horribly as he tried to say the names of his new toys. It was painful for Hunter to watch even now as an adult, because he couldn't understand what his younger self was trying to say. He had to shut it off.

Despite his disfluency, Hunter pursued a career as a lawyer. On his first day of law school, he was called out by a person he describes as a "legendarily tough professor." The teacher pointed at him. "You! Stand up! What's your name? Where are you from?" He was already nervous. He stuttered on the "h" in his first name. "W-w-w-what?" she responded. He tried to hold his composure. "Sorry, ma'am, I have a stutter." The professor was horrified. Later, Hunter's classmates pulled him aside and told him he was their hero for standing up to her.

He eventually landed at a downtown Denver practice that specializes in property law. When it was time to set up his voicemail, he closed the door of his new office and struggled to record an outgoing message. "The walls were super thin, so the people on either side of me must have thought I was nuts, just saying my name over and over and over and over again," he said. "I was in there for a half hour at least. Probably longer than that."

When his future wife, Jessica, brought Hunter home to meet her family, she warned them that he was a stutterer. They welcomed him with open arms, though her youngest brother, who was barely a preteen at the time, didn't know how to react. Whenever Hunter would struggle to speak, Jessica's brother would become visibly uncomfortable. As he got older, he became more at ease with Hunter's disfluency.

Hunter told me he and Jessica designed their wedding so he would have to talk as little as possible. Several years later they had a beautiful baby, Harper.

"Fortunately, she's a girl, and statistically, girls don't stutter as much—but that's one of the things that I'm terrified about. I don't want her to have to go through it," he said. "I still try to read to her every night. I definitely stutter on the words at times, but not as bad as I thought that I would. And then, um, I'm also, uh, going through, um, this is a recent development that I don't think we've talked about . . . I was diagnosed with cancer recently," he said.

About six weeks before our first long conversation, Hunter learned he had stage 4 colon cancer. The first oncologist he saw told him he might have two years to live, six if he was lucky. Jessica, normally emotionally stoic, started bawling when he gave her the news. Hunter had surgery four days later. After waking up, he forced himself to walk around the hospital hallways every hour, despite the pain. He soon started chemotherapy. Doctors installed a port under his skin near his heart. His soft black hair thinned out and turned coarse. A rash started to creep across his chest, stomach, back, and shoulders, then it inched up his neck. The skin on his hands and heels and toes cracked open.

"It's hard seeing it be hard on Jessica," he said. "I feel bad about it. I haven't actively done something to make her feel that way, but it's hard not to feel like it's your fault. But, you know, she is able to handle it pretty well, too. Her parents moved out here a few months ago. They were always planning to move to Colorado, they just expedited it. One of the things cancer's taught me is to learn to accept help, and that's very hard, 'cause I always want to be the person helping people."

He told me how he was struggling to say the names of various chemotherapy drugs, and how he had to tell the nurses and doctors that what they were hearing wasn't a side effect of anesthesia or other drugs, it's just how he talks. He lost some of his dexterity and occasionally would ask Jessica to help him untie a pair of shoes. "I'm very sensitive to the cold," he said. "I was talking with my neighbor for half an hour yesterday, and it was a nice day, like forty-five degrees, and the tip of my nose got so cold it went numb . . . One of the first things I want to do when I get into remission and I recover from the side effects: I want an Oreo milkshake like you cannot believe. I'm dreaming of it," he said.

I told Hunter that during the course of this project I'd been talking to many people who stutter, and that a lot of them had said something along the lines of "You know, it could be worse. I could have cancer." Hunter laughed. Then he said something that genuinely shocked me: that being a person who stutters *prepared* him for cancer.

"I think the reason that I associate the two is because they're invisible," he said. "I mean, obviously with cancer, you can see it through scans, but I can't see it on the outside of me, so it's an invisible fight, an invisible battle. And you know, I shouldn't say 'battle.' It's more of a war, because it's so long," he said. "I have to fight. I have to persevere. I don't have a choice. I have to go through these treatments, I have to last as long as I can. People are like, 'Oh, I'm so proud of your attitude,' and stuff like that. And that's great to hear, but I don't have a choice. I have to be optimistic. If I'm pessimistic, then I get down on myself, and then I get depressed. And if I'm gonna be depressed, then it's gonna take up my days. I don't want however many days I have left filled with self-pity and wallowing. And I attribute some of that attitude to having a stutter for my entire life. I could wallow in self-pity and, you know, find a job where I never talk to people, or I can have a fulfilled life, where you just have to struggle with it sometimes."

As he spoke, I thought a lot about my dad, who has been fighting lymphoma for the past decade. I remember exactly where I was standing on the night I got the call. I was in the parking lot of a roller rink on the outskirts of Penn State, pressing the phone to my right ear, staring off into the darkness. He told me he'd soon be going in for immunotherapy infusions. I told Hunter about my dad and he immediately understood in a way I can't.

"I'm sure that he'll tell you this: having a kid is the biggest motivation you could possibly imagine," Hunter said. His voice changed. Now he was speaking with a mix of reverence and assuredness. "It's like—okay—my wife would be fine. It would be tough, but she'd be fine. My friends would be fine. My parents would be fine. But my daughter would not," he said. "I have great friends and they've been amazing through everything. They've said, 'Hey, if anything happens, Harper will be okay.' But, you know, she needs her dad. Besides wanting to live as long as I can, she's the biggest motivation. Getting to see her after a tough day just makes everything better. And I'm sure that your dad would say the same thing about you."

I asked if he thought any part of his life as a stutterer would change after his experience with cancer. He took his time thinking before beginning to answer.

"I think I won't hold back as much. I will always care that I stutter, but it'll be more of just a part of me, instead of something that I dread, or something that frustrates me. And I'm sure it will still frustrate me at times, I'm not naïve enough to think that. But I think having cancer, especially at a certain age, it teaches you that you're not immortal. If I have to call a person, I think I won't hesitate as much. 'Cause it's like, what's the worst that can happen? I've already been through it."

"It Just Didn't Deter Me"

L ittle by little, the more I embraced stuttering after my Biden story, the more I got to know successful stutterers from all walks of life.

In 2011, the writer Nathan Heller published an eloquent essay in *Slate* about *The King's Speech* and the many layers of the disorder. "I have stuttered nearly all my conscious life, but I still fight the urge to apologize every time it happens," he wrote. He reflected on his own chosen profession: "Writing as a vocation tends to attract control freaks, pathological introverts, and uneasy narcissists—the sort of people, basically, who don't mind spending hours alone at a desk, trying to make their own ideas sound good on a piece of paper—but for stutterers, the endless possibilities for voice control on the blank page carry especial appeal. Give a stutterer a pen and some practice and, suddenly, what seems imperfectible in speech is a few scribblings and crossings-out and rescribblings away."

Heller is now a staff writer at *The New Yorker* at work on his first book. He told me about the way he still senses people losing patience when he's holding up conversation—how listeners stare into their cuticles or study the grain of a table during his blocks. He said he still dreads small talk at dinner parties.

"I often suspect that I'm being invited partly because I'm a

New Yorker writer and I'm expected to have all sorts of clever and witty things to say to enrich the conversation." He paused. "And I very rarely do."

Heller and I talked a lot about the continuous-loop nature of stuttering.

"Whenever you have a block as a stuttering person, there's a kind of a tightening of the leash, and you can't ever escape what you were at five years old," he said. "That's, I think, a difficult thing, psychologically, on a regular basis. And also I think it's relatively unusual among a lot of the challenges that people deal with over the course of their lives. There is a kind of a connection to all of your history with the disorder that you can never completely outrun."

About a decade ago, the British writer Katherine Preston published a moving memoir called *Out With It* about her journey coming to America to meet other stutterers—one of whom she would later marry. I asked Preston what's changed in her life since writing the book. "I got to a point where, having not spoken about my speech for all of my life, all of the sudden it was *all* that I was speaking about," she said with a laugh.

There's no agreed-upon term to describe the moment you start publicly identifying as a person who stutters, though some stutterers I've interviewed have likened it to the experience of coming out. Barry Yeoman, a freelance journalist and teacher at Wake Forest and Duke, has written about the various cultural perceptions of stuttering for decades. In *Psychology Today,* he once described his experience of calling an upscale restaurant only to have the host refuse to take his reservation, because "we don't seat people with speech impediments."

Yeoman told me that he's long viewed his stutter and his sexual orientation through a lens of intersectionality. In the early 1990s he cofounded a stuttering organization called Passing Twice, with the aim of helping LGBTQ stutterers embrace their full identities. In a column for *Out* magazine, Yeoman once wrote, "When I cruised the piers back home in New York, or walked the hallways of the St. Mark's Baths, physical intimacy came easily—because I didn't have to speak. Introduce words into the conversation and everything would fall apart."

"I do think that my coming out as gay informed my making peace with my stutter," Yeoman told me. "Having watched so many people in my life and in the greater world go from a place of shame around their sexualities to a place of real joy and community inspired me so much, and because I think of allyships, I think of finding common ground a lot. I've long wanted to take the lessons of my coming out as a gay man and apply them to other places in my life."

As the months passed, I became more and more aware of an entire population of adults who didn't just *used* to stutter as kids and mercifully "beat it," but people who were still navigating the disorder every day in competitive professional spaces. There's Morgan Housel, the best-selling author of *The Psychology of Money,* who, despite being able to speak before thousands at conferences around the globe, told me he still dreads the moment a flight attendant rolls up to his row with the beverage cart. David Rogier, the CEO and cofounder of MasterClass, told me he prefers to deliver his presentations without a script so he can maneuver around certain sounds or pepper in curse words to help aid his fluency—something he learned from fellow stutterer Samuel L. Jackson. Marc Vetri, a James Beard Award–winning chef, told me about overcoming his fear of ordering ingredients over the phone and having answering machines cut him off during bad blocks. Former

NBA player Michael Kidd-Gilchrist told me that postgame interviews were uncomfortable for him throughout his career, so he started a stuttering charity and is lobbying insurers to cover speech therapy. NFL offensive tackle Brandon Shell described to me the way his classmates used to laugh at him and mock his disfluency to his face. Instead of fighting back, Shell simply owned it. After that, "nobody could hurt me," he said. "Once you have peace with yourself, nobody else matters. Nothing else matters."

And then I met Jeff Zeleny.

ON SEPTEMBER 11, 2001, Zeleny was working in the D.C. bureau of the *Chicago Tribune*. When the news of the terrorist attacks broke, he hailed a cab and raced across the Fourteenth Street bridge to the Pentagon. The car came to a stop and he jumped out and sprinted toward the smoke. His job was to gather as many eyewitness accounts as he could, as fast as he could.

"Whenever you had to do something like that, the adrenaline was running. It was really kind of crazy. I remember trying to slow down, really trying to focus on being fluent as I was giving my dictation to someone back in the Washington bureau," he later told me.

He struggled to find a working cell signal that day. When the call finally went through, he had a flashback to childhood taunts from the playground and three words from his brother: *Spit it out!*

"That was in my mind," he said. "Like I *literally* had to spit it out."

Zeleny grew up in Exeter, Nebraska, a rural town of fewer than six hundred people. As a kid, when he'd try to answer the kitchen phone, he would enter interminable blocks. ("I couldn't say 'Hello,' I couldn't say 'Zelenys.'") He'd eventually hand the receiver off to one of his brothers.

His father, a farmer, never went to college but was an obsessive newshound, something he passed on to his son. Zeleny would make his own newspapers as a kid. He'd park himself in front of the TV, glued to newscasts from his idol, Dan Rather.

Once a week, Zeleny's parents would drive him almost sixty miles each way to the Barkley Speech Language and Hearing Clinic at the University of Nebraska. There, he worked with a therapist who didn't try to erase his stutter but offered effective strategies to help him manage it. Specifically, Zeleny started talking with his hands. Decades later, he still stutters, but he's now chief national affairs correspondent at CNN.

"There are some days when, like, a few reports in a row, or a couple days in a row, or if I'm tired . . . I've always kind of wondered: How bad would it have to get for someone to say something to me? Are the bosses talking privately, like, 'Oh my gosh, he can't, you know, speak'?"

If you watch CNN, you may notice Zeleny moving his hands like an orchestra conductor, pulling certain words toward the camera, guiding himself through the broadcast. Sometimes he subtly dips his head to emphasize a word at the start of a new sentence. The end result is near-total fluency. His dispatches from the field are confident and concise. Still, some viewers mock what's left of his stutter online.

"If you would have reached out to me five years ago, I probably would have been horrified to even acknowledge it or talk about it," he said. "When I went to ABC for two years, I was afraid that people were going to find out. I guess it was a test for myself, like, would I be able to do this?"

He told me that stuttering has made him more comfortable with long silences. He works hard to be patient and a better listener—two traits that have served him as a journalist.

"I guess I would like to say, 'Oh, I channeled it into working harder and, you know, focused on my goals,' but that's a little more grandiose than is probably true," he said. "Next week, when I'm on TV, I'm sure I'll have some type of an issue, and I'll probably be mad at myself momentarily." Still, he never viewed stuttering as an excuse to opt out. "It just didn't deter me," he said.

THREE MONTHS AFTER my article came out, I went back to my high school, where one of my classmates, Kevin, is teaching English. I hadn't seen him in many years, but he looked the same, save for the flecks of gray hair sprouting on the sides of his head. (Same goes for me.) Kevin and I walked through the hallways, past our class photo framed on one of the cream-colored walls. In the teachers' lounge he poured me a cup of burnt coffee in an old blue mug, then we moseyed down to his classroom.

He's a cool teacher. His walls are littered with torn *New Yorker* covers alongside images of Kurt Vonnegut, A Tribe Called Quest, and Minor Threat. When we were teenagers, Kevin was one of the few guys in class who remained sober. He didn't make a big deal of it, he just drank ginger ale at parties and in general liked hanging out at all-night diners more than standing around the keg in the field. It was always his dream to become a high school English teacher, and, if possible, at our alma mater. It worked out.

We took our seats at the front of the room and Kevin introduced me to his class. Mr. Braithwaite, our old religion teacher, snuck in the back door and smiled at me as he sat down at an empty desk. The overhead lights were harsher than I remembered, but barely anything else had changed. The blackboard was still dusty, with that week's homework assignments written in the corner. The pencil sharpener was bolted to the wall by the door, with the same little trash can positioned below to catch the shavings.

As Kevin interviewed me about my career, I felt myself watching the scene from above. I had been in this same classroom fifteen years ago, sitting in one of those desks, terrified of having to speak. There were many days I doubted that I'd ever be able to hold a job. Now I was here to offer students advice.

23

"A Softer Place to Land"

Before receiving those Biden story emails, I never considered myself a member of the "stuttering community." I didn't even know there *was* a stuttering community. Stuttering was always my thing, my issue, my problem, my lonely journey. I was on an island with it and I didn't expect anyone to understand. So many of the people who wrote to me didn't consider themselves members of the stuttering community either. I heard from many stutterers who are still trying to conceal their disfluency from their friends and coworkers. A lot of emails started the same way: "I've never told anybody this, but . . ."

On the opposite end of the spectrum are the stutterers who show up each month at a local chapter meeting of the National Stuttering Association (NSA) or a similar group. Several stutterers encouraged me to check out one of the Manhattan or Brooklyn meetings, but it took a full nine months before I felt ready to go. I had spent my whole life trying to be *more than* just a person with this problem, clinging to this idea that I could sometimes pass for "normal." Going to a stuttering support group felt like giving up on that illusion once and for all.

The first time I attended was a hot Monday night in July. I needed to crack a beer even though the meeting was taking place over Zoom. I nervously clicked the link. At first, it was strange to watch other people stutter, even on video. I saw their jerking heads, their constricted chests, and I felt . . . bad. I still wrestle with this sometimes. In my weakest moments, I want someone else's block to be over, just like I want mine to be over, and that makes me a hypocrite. I *hate* when people pity me and I hate that I might be pitying someone else.

At the start of each chapter meeting, one stutterer reads the opening words. It's a few paragraphs about how these next two hours are a safe space, a place to practice your techniques or to just stutter openly, a room free of fear and judgment. Then we all introduce ourselves. It's not quite like AA, but there's an understanding that these meetings are more or less off the record. I don't know where I looked or what I said when it was my turn. I couldn't stare at the little green webcam light. When it was over I quietly wondered if I'd made the others in the room uncomfortable.

Spring Kwok co-leads the Manhattan chapter. She is in her late twenties and has a soft, calming voice. She almost smiles when she stutters. Spring told the room about how her boss was recently attempting to make accommodations for her at work. I asked if this felt kind or infantilizing. "Um, a mix of both," she said. She was working hard to maintain eye contact with the camera during her particularly long blocks. At one point she said, "I'm having trouble breathing right now." Everyone at the meeting nodded.

Zoom is still a nightmare for me. Something about the little boxes makes me feel extremely tense and on the spot. It's like being back in elementary school. I have to fight that sinking feeling that when I block I'm taking up too much of everyone's time. Every now and then I hear a sentence from a fellow stutterer that crystallizes something I've long struggled to articulate myself. A nurse practitioner named Roísín McManus told me that, growing up, whenever she was battling a sentence, her mother would look away with a pained expression—or, as Roísín put it, "like I was stabbing her in the stomach."

Roísín (pronounced *Ro-Sheen*) grew up in a culturally Catholic family of five in Rhode Island. Her stutter would most often manifest in the form of prolonged repetitions. "My parents are very nice, loving people, but they just took a very disciplinarian approach to stuttering," she later told me. Some nights she'd pray for it to go away. Other times she'd threaten to stop speaking at all. As we talked one on one, she became fired up when telling me stories of her early years.

"I've had many times in my life where I've felt a lot of anger towards the stuttering industrial complex—speech therapists, doctors, teachers, and parents—all aligning their own interests against the interests of a kid who stutters," she said. "It was like, 'Just hide it. Just hide that you're struggling. And on top of hiding the stuttering, now hide that it's even a problem for you.' It was such a trap."

As her childhood years passed, Roísín came to know her stutter intimately. She could anticipate periods of severe disfluency hours ahead of time. Whenever her parents tried to bring up her problem, she'd melt down and sometimes literally run away from the conversation. Things got worse as she moved through high school. "I was starting to go to parties and think about sexuality and flirting with people, and drugs, and I just felt so much pressure to get this under control, and I had nobody to help me with it," she said. "I wouldn't open up to anybody about it, because opening up felt like a mine field."

Roísín has soulful hazel eyes. She's the type of person who comes across as a natural caretaker. Her mom is a surgeon and her aunt has worked as a midwife and counselor. Roísín initially set out to study social work but felt called to nursing. In college, her stutter appeared to be standing in the way of her dream. As an undergrad at NYU, she spent countless days and nights trudging around Lower Manhattan thinking: *I'm never gonna stop stuttering. I'll never be able to hold a job.* Her disorder was dominating her life like never before.

"I was told by one interviewer that he would hire me if I didn't have a stutter," she said. "He was like, 'Thank you for everything you said, but we're just worried about the patients, and their comfort level, and if you didn't stutter, we would hire you in a heartbeat, but I'm sure you're gonna find something.'"

When she was twenty-one, Roísín turned her life upside down. For the first time, she attempted to allow herself to stutter openly in conversation. She soon began showing up at monthly NSA meetings. Each time she entered the room, she could feel herself let go. One of the chapter leaders at the time, Eric S. Jackson, who went on to become an assistant professor of communicative sciences and disorders at NYU, helped her reframe the problem. Eric introduced her to other stutterers around the city and encouraged her to advertise her disfluency as much as possible. The two of them even dated for a little while. But outside of her little stuttering bubble, the transformation was rockier.

"If you think about the metaphor of coming out of the closet, like, from telling one person about it and talking about it to living a life where I wasn't hiding it—that was a two-year process," she said.

"My dad was so happy for me. He was so proud of me that I could own this thing about myself and be an advocate for other people," she said. "With my mom, it was more painful. She really was scared that my decision to accept it was going to doom me. I told her 'fix it' is not an option for me, but she didn't understand that. As I was 'coming out' and trying to stutter openly, we had screaming, terrible fights. It was all her fear for me. It was very painful."

Roísín kept pushing forward. Within a few years, she had become an NSA chapter co-leader herself and was attending stuttering conventions all over the country. Even though her relationship with her mother remained strained, she'd later learn that her mom was cheering her on from a distance.

"I was on stuttering podcasts and she wouldn't talk to me about it, but she would send my podcasts to my brother and be, like, 'Roísín is doing so well, isn't this so amazing?'"

One night I asked Roísín's mom, Betty, what she wished she'd known about stuttering back when Roísín was becoming a teenager. She likened Roísín's stutter to a family secret—"and secrets tend to not be good," Betty said. She paused. "They tend to kind of close us down."

"It would have been nice if I could have in some way helped her with what must have been a lot of inner turmoil that she didn't share with us," she said. "Maybe that's a normal part of development when you're a teenager, not sharing things with your parents. But it would have been nice if I could have been more accepting."

STAVROS LADEAS, a software developer from the Poconos, went to great lengths to hide his disorder from even his closest family members. "Covert stutterers" like Stavros are able to get by with constant word switching as they navigate sentences.

"Even my brother, who I was pretty close with growing up, when I began talking about needing to go to speech therapy, he was surprised," Stavros told me.

After moving to New York and working with clinicians at the American Institute for Stuttering, Stavros decided to join the local NSA chapter. One night he went out for drinks with a group of fellow stutterers and noticed a tall brunette in the corner—Roísín. He had never met a woman who stuttered with a mix of openness and confidence like her. She didn't seem ashamed of her problem, and he didn't know what to make of it. They kept seeing each other at various stuttering events, and formed a close friendship. A few years later, at a stuttering conference in Arizona, Stavros summoned the courage to ask her out. As a couple, they immediately understood each other in profound ways.

"If we're at a restaurant and one of us is stuttering a lot, and someone points it out, there's just a softer place to land," Roísín told me. "I don't feel wounded for him in the way that I would if I didn't stutter."

Stavros is the son of Greek immigrants, and he and Roísín had planned to get married on a Greek island in the summer of 2020, but the pandemic indefinitely delayed the ceremony. One week before Christmas that year, Roísín woke up with an idea. She called two friends and told them to come to Prospect Park, not far from their apartment in Brooklyn. She put a simple shawl over her wedding dress and wore black long johns underneath. Stavros dressed in a handsome suit and duck boots. The two of them walked across crunchy white snow holding hands. Family members watched the impromptu ceremony over a livestream. A bottle of champagne sat wedged in the snow.

Given that stuttering has a strong genetic component, I

asked Roísín if she ever thinks about the prospect of raising a child who ends up having the disorder. She didn't seem worried.

"We know all these great people, and we have all these resources to help a kid who stutters," she said. "But you never know how someone is going to experience stuttering, and if we're the parents that are like, 'It's cool, accept it, we all stutter,' the kid might totally rebel against that." And then she laughed. The summer after the wedding, Roísín gave birth to a baby girl, Clio. She'll start talking soon.

24

"There Is No *Yet*"

I would love to talk to your mom," Dr. Courtney Byrd told me. "And help her try to understand that she did the best that she could do with what she was given."

Dr. Byrd is a professor at the University of Texas at Austin, where she runs the country's preeminent stuttering research center. She's a bit of an outlaw in her field. She likes to ask her fellow speech therapists a rhetorical question, though it can also be read as a direct challenge: "At what point are we going to look at our therapy and say, 'Where are all these people who benefited from fluency-shaping?'"

Dr. Byrd is not shy about railing against the therapists who make thousands of dollars, as she puts it, "exploiting" the various myths about stuttering.

"I believe—and this is where I get controversial—that a lot of the stigma that's related to stuttering begins in the office of the speech-language pathologist," she said. "You can't tell a child that it's okay to stutter while also telling them that they need to get to a percentage of fluency that is not possible, even for people who don't stutter." She brought up how so many therapists are hesitant to even say the word "stuttering" to the parents of their patients.

A few years ago, the stutterer Arthur Blank, owner of the

Atlanta Falcons and cofounder of Home Depot, established a $20 million legacy grant to support and expand Dr. Byrd's work at UT Austin. Usually these types of donations come with grand pronouncements like "end stuttering." But over the past twenty-five years, Dr. Byrd has treated thousands of patients, and she tells them all the same thing: *There is no cure for this.* She wants young stutterers and their families to understand that truth before they even begin working with her.

"If you look at the cognitive behavioral psychology literature, you can have one noxious event, and that one noxious event can change the entire course of your life," she said. "And I strongly believe that we have an ethical responsibility to educate these children about how they talk. We need to be thinking about this child when they're forty, and what can we do for them now? And if all we're doing is focusing on fluency, then we're setting them up for failure in a way that I think we're responsible for."

She told me a story about one of her patients, a four-year-old girl, going to the dentist to get her teeth cleaned. The little girl stuttered when trying to introduce herself to the doctor at the start of the visit. The dentist looked down at her. *W-w-w-what? Did you forget your name?* Every young stutterer knows this scene. You look over at your mom, whose face has fallen to her feet. You look back at the dentist. You don't really know what to say. Of course you didn't forget your name. You know it better than any other word, because you stutter on it more than any other word. In the world Dr. Byrd is working to create, the little girl *knows* she stutters and feels no shame for it. It's just one part of her.

"When children have AIDS, or they have cancer, if the doctor just tells them, 'This is what you have,' the child's anxiety surrounding the diagnosis is much lower, if it even exists. The child is much more likely to ask questions about it. The parents are much more likely to ask questions and feel comfortable with it. And the parent and the child, importantly, are much more likely to talk to each other about it. I have worked with thousands of people who stutter, and they don't ever say, 'If only everyone would have just ignored my stuttering, if only no one would have talked to me about it, if only I could go back in that speech therapy room and spend more time on how to say those words, I know my life would be so much better.'"

As an undergrad, Dr. Byrd was struck by the way her professors didn't seem to understand stuttering at all. One of her earliest patients, a thirteen-year-old boy, told her that the moment he walked out of the treatment room, everything she taught him went away. He would practice fluency-shaping strategies at home with a tape recorder and bring it in for her to listen. He was totally disfluent. She raised the problem to her supervisor, who blamed the teenager. The boy soon started to cry during his sessions.

"The only response I had for him was what I was taught, and that was just 'You've got to practice more.' It still haunts me to this day, really. But it set my life on a path to try to figure it out."

EVEN NOW, YEARS LATER, Meghan Kleon can get emotional when talking about the day she received the news. She was picking up her son Owen from preschool and a member of the school staff pulled her into an office. Meghan was informed that teachers at the school couldn't understand her son and that she needed to address the issue. When she got back to her car, she burst into tears. She immediately called her husband, Austin, who was out of town. He went into a rage.

"We were pissed," Austin later told me. "We were like, 'Fuck you! He's fine! He's brilliant! Why are you making this a thing?'" This was a private preschool, and the Kleons were stunned at what they felt was a lack of tact and nuance. "That was the first time another adult said to us, 'There's something wrong with your kid,'" Austin said.

Meghan, for her part, was devastated.

"I want to protect him so much. And as a mother, I blamed myself, especially at that time. I didn't know much about stuttering. 'Is it my parenting? Is it something I've done wrong?' It made me so angry, because I knew that Owen was this amazing, interesting kid, and the fact that anyone could look at him and essentially just boil him down to the way that he speaks was infuriating to me," she said. "We ended up pulling him out of that school because of that experience."

Soon, a speech therapist started coming to their house for private sessions.

"I didn't know how to talk to Owen about it," Meghan said. "I often danced around it and would say, 'Oh, we're gonna talk to somebody who's gonna talk to you about speech and talking and language,' and leave it very vague."

Owen's first therapist relied mainly on worksheets and used a fluency-shaping approach. It didn't work. Meghan said the therapist seemed to reiterate the school's messaging: that Owen needed to be *fixed*. Around that time, one of Meghan's friends heard a local radio segment about a program at nearby UT, focused exclusively on helping people who stutter. Meghan drove Owen to campus for an evaluation. Soon, he began working with Dr. Byrd's team.

Dr. Byrd didn't mince words when she met the Kleons: she wanted them to know that Owen was *aware* that he sounded different from other people, and that, as parents, they needed to articulate that to him.

"It was just—it was life-changing," Meghan told me. "It literally was not until that happened that I was able to talk to him about his stuttering."

When Owen entered the UT program, Dr. Byrd's team asked him a series of questions—namely about how he *felt* about the way he talked. Owen said he sometimes felt like people interrupted him and didn't let him finish his thoughts. He could also tell people thought he didn't speak the right way.

"That was not unexpected, but it's still so hard as a parent to hear," Meghan said.

Dr. Byrd's team stressed to Owen that successful communication is not defined by fluency. They focused on building up his nonverbal skills, such as eye contact, strong posture, and effective body language. They led Owen in desensitizing exercises—sometimes he would stutter into a video camera or speak to passersby at the student union. Crucially, Owen was taught to self-identify as a stutterer.

"You need to talk about it, but you've got to talk about it in a way where you're not apologizing for it," Dr. Byrd said. She told me about her team's study on "apologetic" versus "informative" self-disclosure. Most kids are taught, by parents and therapists, to use language that acknowledges their stutter as an inconvenience: *I'm in therapy, please bear with me, I'm working on it.* Dr. Byrd's research shows that type of language makes people view the stutterer more negatively.

"People don't think you can do jobs that require significant communication, and they want to escape the exchange with you, because they think that you want to," she said. "But, when you can look at them and say you stutter, in a neutral, matter-of-fact way, and you keep moving forward, people can't even tell you how much you stuttered in the exchange."

She said that her team follows their patients longitudinally, and that the majority of them report a significantly lower degree of bullying, depression, and anxiety than those who learn only fluency-shaping techniques.

In time, Meghan watched Owen become comfortable standing up for himself when someone talked over him or, worse, mocked his disfluency. "I've seen him do it," she said proudly.

Owen's dad, Austin, is the author of *Steal Like An Artist,* a meditation on creativity that doubles as a self-help manual. As Austin has watched Owen grow up, his perspective on stuttering has changed. In conversation, Austin may describe his son's stutter as "incredible" or "profound" or other notably positive adjectives.

"It definitely has a real rhythm to it," he said. He and Owen both play piano, and their house is filled with musical instruments. Around the age of four, Owen started messing around with his dad's synthesizer. He was soon making electronic music that utilized "stuttering" sounds.

One year over the holidays, Owen's stutter shifted from steady repetitions to intense blocks. Meghan told me it seemed like her son was choking on words trying to get them out—that his stutter suddenly felt *violent.*

"As enlightened as we felt like we were at the time, that is something we freaked out about," Austin admitted.

He and Meghan called Dr. Byrd, who tried to talk them off the ledge.

"She was like, 'This happens a lot, don't worry about it.'" She wanted them to know that stuttering is variable in nature, that things like this would keep happening. Owen's stutter eventually returned to its old musical form.

"I think parents are so worried about difference," Austin said. "But there's something wider going on in our culture about difference and disability. I feel very lucky. Of all the shit show that the contemporary world is, I feel that it's a great time to have a child with a difference. Having a child with a difference expands you as a person. I'm cooler with kids with quirks now. I'm cooler with people with all kinds of differences now, because it's expanded my world a little bit more."

He spoke tenderly about the way that Owen has developed a strong sense of self over the past few years.

"The other thing that I've picked up from being his dad is that you can't isolate anything in anybody's life," Austin said. "It's all part of the whole." He said his family's positive experience with the stuttering institute at UT is one of the many reasons they've remained in the region. "I said to Dr. Byrd, 'Well, you know, he just hasn't been beaten down yet.' And she said, 'There is no *yet*. If we do what we're doing, and we keep doing it, there is no *yet*.'"

FOR THE BETTER PART of a decade, Dr. Byrd lobbied the Austin Independent School District to change its guidelines for accommodations for students who stutter. Rather than advocate for increased classroom flexibility, Dr. Byrd convinced the school district that stutterers should be treated like every other student. In a practical sense, that means children who stutter are still required to present in class and to read out loud. They also may be called on at random and expected to respond like all of their fellow classmates. It's a counterintuitive approach, particularly as the disability rights movement has spent years pushing for *more* accommodation in public spaces. But this gets back to her animating idea: given that there is no "cure" for stuttering, it's up to therapists, educators, parents, and other authority figures to empower children who stutter to live full lives.

"Stutterers go years upon years upon years with never having had the same pragmatic developmental opportunities that their peers have, and yet they're thrust into it at the college level with minimal to no practice, with a history of experiences that have made them feel less than, not as good, not capable," she said.

I thought back to my endless chain of public-speaking emails during my senior year at Penn State, that avoidance that nearly cost me my diploma. I thought about how Ms. Samson had pulled me aside in elementary school and, with the best of intentions, told me to let her know whenever I felt uncomfortable with a verbal assignment. I thought about the way the first ring of the house phone always made the hair on my arms stand up. As I'm writing this, I'm thinking about the fact that I've never had the courage to leave an outgoing message on my iPhone.

"For some people, you have no choice but to be who you are; for others, you spend a lifetime hiding who you are, because people tell you that you can't be who you want to be if you can't be that person fluently," Dr. Byrd said. "I see it in teens and adults who I work with. There's so much self-harm. There are so many things that they say to themselves, and a lot of those voices sometimes even come from their closest family members. We have to learn how to change the language, change what we say to ourselves. It's not only about acceptance; it's about mindfulness, it's about understanding, it's about self-compassion: *What are the voices inside my head?*"

She offered a metaphor from Dr. Steven C. Hayes, the psychologist who developed Acceptance and Commitment Therapy. Hayes tries to remind people that the voices in your head are like passengers on a bus: You can't get rid of them, and in some cases, you can't even silence them. They may be riding with you for the rest of your life. But at the end of the day, you're the one driving the bus.

As we talked, I remembered how Meghan Kleon said she initially blamed herself for Owen's problem. And I thought about how guilty I sensed my own mom felt for the way she handled my stutter, and how I don't want her to carry that weight. I told Dr. Byrd this.

"She couldn't have known anything different," Dr. Byrd said. "If someone tells you, 'These are the things that we can do and your child will be fluent,' of course you're going to do that. I mean, you'll do anything to protect your child. And let me say: the teachers and the parents who don't talk about it, and the speech-language pathologists, they're trying to protect the child. It's not out of a place of harm. But I think of that group, the speech-language pathologist has to have the courage to say, 'There is another way.'"

25

Mom and Dad

I pulled into my parents' driveway and flicked off the engine. It was late September, and the tree out front was turning a golden yellow. My dad was sitting on the porch in his usual navy sweater and white button-down, a newspaper splayed across the lap of his baggy khakis. My mom came out to greet me in a periwinkle blouse with a silk scarf around her neck. It was just after lunch; she knew I hadn't eaten. She had a Wawa hoagie and a slew of beverages waiting for me on a little table: Vitaminwater, lemonade, Diet Coke. I said thank you and scarfed down the sandwich and we made small talk about my drive from New York. We sat facing each other on opposite sides of the front porch. We were all afraid to bring it up, the real reason why I was there: to finally talk about this thing we had never discussed.

"They gave me brochures," my mom said flatly. "And they, uh, recommended that if we were a family of interrupters, to slow down, give you time to finish your sentences, establish eye contact with you when you were talking."

My mom leaned forward in her white wicker chair as she spoke. Her eyes were drooping and sad, not the reservoir of warmth I was used to. I could hardly blame her. Now my mind was racing with questions: *Is this even fair? Why am I putting this in a book? To have people feel sorry for me? Why does my family have to be the sacrificial lamb? Did they ever agree to that?* Nobody signed a pledge twenty years ago saying, "Okay, we'll meet here to hash it out one day!" I love my parents, and I love my brother, and I don't want to do anything to upset them. I don't want my mom and dad to feel like they failed or to spend the last years of their lives filled with regret. I viewed the fact that my parents and I were here—that they were willing to let me interview them—as an expression of their love, and I was so grateful for it.

I had appeared in a PBS documentary about Biden a few nights earlier, and my mom's sisters and friends had been reaching out to her to talk about it. I was notably disfluent throughout my short segment; my throat gulped and spasmed as I fought to stare at the camera and describe Biden's stutter. It was hard for me to watch—I can only imagine how hard it was for my parents. I eventually asked them.

"What is it like to watch you stutter? Well, my heart fills up with pride at your grit," my mom said.

We talked about how I had cycled through almost half a dozen therapists before finally reaching Joe, and how none of the techniques I ever learned seemed to work.

"There was this term called 'easy onset' that they were pushing," my mom said. "When I would remind you to use it and take a deep breath, you didn't like it, and it was almost like you'd forget about the rest of the sentence. And what I should have realized was: *This is hard enough for John.* In retrospect, you didn't need those reminders, because you were living it on a visceral level."

We were fifteen minutes in and it was already the longest we'd ever spoken about any of this stuff. I finally asked why it seemed like we couldn't even *say* "stutter" in the house. "Did you think the word would hurt me?" I asked.

"Coming from me?" my mom asked. My dad interjected before she could finish.

"I, at least, took the signals from you that you didn't want to discuss it," he said. "I thought if I ever said to you the word 'stutter,' it would be something that you would have not wanted me to say. That's how I read it."

I wanted to ask a follow-up question, but I also wanted to wait and give them time to reflect. I could see the wheels turning in my mom's head. She peered out at the dogwood tree.

"I can look at my childhood and, culturally, I can say that my family did not address things head-on," she said. "For example, apparently when I was about two, maybe three, I started pulling my hair out. Uncle John brought this up to me once. He said, 'If you had a child who was pulling their hair out today, you would take them to the doctor, you would take them to therapy.' What my parents did is they cut my hair short—that's how they dealt with it."

I had never heard this story. I thought about all the late nights I used to sit out on this porch drinking and smoking weed, wanting to be anywhere but here. I pictured that first summer we moved in, just after I finished eighth grade, before I entered high school. I spent a lot of time in my room, the only place where I wouldn't have to talk—or think—about my stutter. And of course I thought about it anyway.

"Why didn't I have the courage, the wherewithal, to knock on your door?" my dad asked. He was upset with himself. "I mean, what was the worst that could have happened? You would have said, 'Get out of my room, Dad, I don't want to talk about this.'"

He was sitting with his arms crossed. His face was low. I

could tell he felt bad, but I didn't want him to beat himself up. He turned the interview on me and asked why I never wanted to talk about it. "Was pride part of it? Or what?" he asked. "Again, I have plenty of regrets. I have many places I had to have been stronger and I was not. I will stand up in court and that's the first thing I will say. But I also would like to say, What was your motivation? Why were all the signals 'Don't ask me about this'?"

I didn't know what to say. I was taken aback by his use of "court." The last thing I wanted was for either of them to feel like they were on the witness stand.

"One of the burdens I've . . . been under . . . this past year is to be . . . Zen master, the stuttering guru. And to . . . play the part of self-actualized," I began. "And I'm not. And a . . . big part of this book is . . . I'm trying to . . . figure these things out."

The more we talked, the easier the conversation got. My mom reminded me that, not long after I started working with Joe, he suggested I go away to a six-week intensive therapy program in Iowa. "I remember this profoundly," she said. "You said to me, 'I'm worried about going and coming back and things are still the same.' That really showed me a whole other level of the weight that you carry."

I had conveniently blacked out that memory, just like I'd blacked out the night I first met Sam's parents, when I could barely say a word without contorting.

As the three of us spoke that afternoon, I thought about all the ways my parents had tried to protect me growing up, for better or worse. My mom constantly ordered for me at restaurants, even though I never asked her to. On my first morning of ninth grade, she drove me to school rather than have me take the bus with new kids.

"I'll never forget watching you walk down that main walk,"

she said. "But I think of so many risks you took. Do you look back and feel good about yourself? Or are you sitting there thinking, 'You don't know what I didn't do, what I chose not to participate in'?" I thought for a moment. I told her it was a little bit of both.

My dad said that he always thought I would eventually stop stuttering; my mom was less sure. I asked my dad what it was like after I had graduated from college, knowing I was now out in the real world talking this way. "I began to sober up," he said. "I began to have more compassion. It was as if I was paying lip service for so many years to how hard it must have been for you."

We had been talking for a while now, and both of my parents had said things I never thought I'd hear them say. I was humbled and impressed with their honesty. It also felt a little surreal that we were actually doing this. Nevertheless, we were keeping the conversation in relatively safe territory: not one of us was bringing up Matt. I finally cracked. I asked if they had ever considered sending him away to military school. They said they hadn't. I could see the pain in my mom's eyes.

"You know what, John, if I were you looking back on childhood, and the trauma you've dealt with, I would be really pissed at my parents for not being able to manage my older brother," she said. "I would feel very disappointed and angry, because you're a kid, you're vulnerable. It would mystify me. And I don't have a . . . I don't have an answer. When a brush fire occurred, we put it out with a small extinguisher, and then put out the next brush fire and the next brush fire."

My dad scrunched his face. He nodded. I could tell he was conflicted.

"Every day was like a tornado. Matt, too, knew it was a tornado. This is the devil's dilemma—because it's not as if we're dealing with a bad person," he said. "He hated the way he would explode and couldn't help himself from exploding."

My dad said he has a stack of handwritten apology notes from my brother "this thick"—he held his fingers two inches apart. He told me he keeps the torn sheets of loose-leaf in his bedside table and reads them periodically: *I'm so sorry what I did tonight, please forgive me, I'll start over tomorrow, I don't know why I act like this. I love you so much.*

My mom asked if I was planning to talk to Matt before I finished this project.

"I very much would like to," I said. "But I don't know if he would be open to that."

26

If Not for You

Liz and I spent the holidays together that year—just the two of us. It was the first winter of the pandemic; traveling to see either of our families indoors felt too risky. On Thanksgiving, we watched the Macy's parade in bed. Liz spent all afternoon preparing a beautiful dinner: turkey and mashed potatoes and yams and cranberries and butternut squash and beet salad. We sat at the kitchen table and listened to Ray Charles, then slept late on Black Friday and had leftover apple pie for breakfast. A Christmas tree vendor had already popped up across the street. Liz propped the front door open while I carried a sappy Fraser fir up through our apartment stairwell. As the sun went down, we strung lights across the living room. Liz had tracked down a pair of red stockings with our first initials on them as a surprise. We hung ornaments and took pictures and I leafed through magazines while she practiced "Jingle Bell Rock" on the guitar.

About a week before Christmas, snow blanketed the city. We pulled our boots out of the back of the hall closet and wandered our neighborhood under yellow streetlights. Everyone was home; almost all of the apartments were glowing. We gawked at our neighbors' trees and decorations. The next morning we went sledding until our fingers and toes were numb. We watched *White Christmas* and *Miracle on 34th Street* and *The Muppet Christmas Carol* and just about every other holiday movie right up through Christmas Eve. On Christmas morning we FaceTimed our parents and my nephews and felt the distance more than ever.

Our days fell into a peaceful rhythm that winter. The apartment echoed with the same array of sounds: the whir of the exercise bike, three beeps of the oven timer, clinking metal zippers against the wall of the dryer. We watched a never-ending stream of Bravo reality shows and Ken Burns documentaries. We took long, quiet walks around the park. We'd go to bed early on weekends or stay up late on weeknights for no reason. Liz made pots of chicken soup and trays of chocolate chip cookies. She mastered my mom's beef stew recipe. I tried to read and write as much as I could. We were so grateful not to be sick.

I had known for a while that I wanted to marry her, but for whatever reason, I was scared to talk to Liz's parents about it. Something told me they wouldn't think I was good enough. I psyched myself up for weeks to make the call, then finally asked for their blessing and they said of course without a moment of hesitation. We talked about the first time I was at their house, that Passover when I struggled to read aloud with everyone at the table. I thanked them for welcoming me into their family from that moment, for not judging me, for not thinking less of me. Her mom smiled and cried and said she was so happy Liz and I had found each other.

We flew out to California on Mother's Day weekend. It was the first time we had seen her family in a year. One morning we drove up Sunset Boulevard then veered off for a hike at Will Rogers State Park. After we hit the summit, we sat on a wooden bench and looked out at the Pacific Ocean. I turned to

Liz and told her I loved her. I said something about how she had made me a better person. When I reached into my backpack and took out the ring, she smiled and cried and pulled me in for a long kiss.

I can't really describe how much Liz has done for me. From that first night at the bar when she told me about her journey with dystonia, I've been in awe of her strength. She can talk about her disorder so nonchalantly with both friends and strangers. She exudes her own comfort with the topic, allowing others to feel comfortable with it in return. She's been by my side as I've tried to get better discussing everything related to stuttering.

And then there are all her little things. She still reads my drafts out loud to me because she knows I hate the way my voice breaks the rhythm of a sentence. She's always there to rub my neck when my muscles throb after a day of painful blocks. But more than comfort, more than companionship, more than love, Liz has given me the gift of acceptance. I don't know how I'll ever repay her for that. When I look back at my life, I don't see it as before and after facing my stutter; I see it as before and after meeting Liz. She has allowed me to see the whole me, and to stop running from it.

FOUR MONTHS AFTER I proposed to her, we were back in Los Angeles. Liz needed to have another round of surgery. The battery in her chest was once again dying, and her muscles had been contracting and spasming for weeks. She couldn't walk more than a few blocks without wincing. I'd massage her legs and the arches of her feet to try to take some of the pain away, but it barely helped. She was hurting all over. Her doctors were now encouraging her to switch to a rechargeable battery. If she did this, and if we were lucky, the new device would last a decade, but she'd have to use a large portable apparatus and essentially plug herself in each night. This gave her pause. We weighed the pros and cons of the rechargeable ad nauseam. Ultimately, she decided to go for it.

The day of the surgery, I set my alarm for four thirty in the morning. Liz rolled over and I could feel that her whole body was tense. She hadn't been able to sleep for weeks. We brushed our teeth and threw on clothes and tiptoed through her parents' kitchen. The last time she'd had surgery, I'd sat with her mom and dad in the waiting room. This time, because of the pandemic, each patient was allowed to have only one person accompany them. Liz chose me. Her parents came downstairs in their bathrobes to say I love you, then we drove in the pitch-black toward Cedars-Sinai.

We parked and walked across the sky bridge and took the elevator up to the fifth floor of the hospital. We were the youngest people in the waiting room by about forty years. A nurse eventually called Liz back to preop to change into a hospital gown and those thick yellow socks. About a half hour later, I was allowed back to see her before she went under. The moment I walked in, I could tell something had gone wrong. There was a breathing tube up her nose and the IV was wrapped with layers of tape and bandages. She's always had difficulty around needles and, this time, she had passed out when they went to put it in. When they finally wheeled her toward the operating room, I stuttered, "I lll-love y-you, baby," then watched her disappear down the long corridor. I took a slow walk around the perimeter of the building, trying to clear my mind. I bought a coffee and prayed that this would be our last time at a hospital for a while.

Eventually I was escorted back to the recovery room. I rounded a corner and saw her at a distance. I immediately smiled. The nurse brought over a little cup of apple juice with a small plastic straw that I held to Liz's mouth. She still had all the wires stuck to her body, but the color had returned to her face. I stood next to her bed and held her hand and rubbed her shoulder. Her hair was frizzy and stringy from the blue hairnet. I texted her parents and siblings and my family to let them know she was okay. After a while, the nurse had her get up and try walking around. A staff member put her in a wheelchair and led us down to the parking garage. I drove home extra slow. As we were pulling onto Liz's street, I told her how the woman who had called me back to the recovery room had used the phrase "your wife," and how I hadn't corrected her. Liz smiled.

27

Friends

A little sliver of water cuts through the huge gray rocks under the wooden planks of a footbridge. One by one, stutterers take turns walking up to a microphone just before the bridge. I don't want to speak, but before I know it, I'm heading toward the line. It feels like an invisible force is pushing me forward. I never imagined I'd be here.

I'm surrounded by kids and teens and therapists, but also adults like me—lifelong stutterers who were too ashamed to go to something like this when we were growing up. Now we're all in a group at the closing ceremony of an annual gathering of Friends: The National Association of Young People Who Stutter. It's a nonprofit that was founded in the late 1990s by Lee Caggiano, a speech therapist and mother of a stutterer, and John Ahlbach, an early member of the National Stuttering Project, which later became the National Stuttering Association.

I told myself that I was going to Friends only as an observer. For three days, I roamed the halls of the convention, taking everything in. I had done the same thing a week earlier at the NSA conference, where I dutifully listened to stuttering research presentations. I leaned against the ballroom doors and watched Dr. Byrd deliver a keynote address in which she all but told her peers that they were guilty of malpractice.

At Friends, shortly before our walk to the bridge, we were instructed to write a few reflections on a piece of paper. My mind flashed to what a twenty-two-year-old stutterer, Grace, had said earlier in the week. Grace was sitting center stage on a six-person panel called "How We Want the World to See Us." She turned the prompt, and the larger theme of stuttering empowerment, on its head.

"When we think about stuttering, we think it's bad, but we don't own that, we just cover it up with this toxic positivity, and I don't think that's fair," Grace began. Several parents shuffled nervously in their seats. "When I think about how I want the world to see me, the answer is: I don't know. I know how I *don't* want them to see me. I don't want them to see me the way I see myself."

Grace passed the microphone to Tammy, the mother of a stutterer.

"Lee asked me if I would speak about how I want the world to see my son, and immediately when she asked me that, I had two feelings," Tammy said. "My heart swelled, because I get to talk about my son, who I absolutely adore. And then on the other hand, my heart sank, because this is something I think about every single day, with my son being a stutterer, and my son being a Black man, a Black boy." She glanced toward a corner of the room. "And when you have someone that you adore with immutable traits, you want just for them to be seen at all."

Friends has a bottom-up approach, with young people leading many of the roundtables and workshops. In some ways, the adult stutterers who come to Friends are living vicariously through the kids, watching them run around and stutter freely. We're supposed to be the mentors, but all week long I felt like I was learning more from them.

Many speech therapists also make the trek to Friends. Chaya Goldstein, a therapist from the American Institute for Stuttering, delivered a presentation about trauma-informed therapy. In addition to being a therapist, Chaya is a person who stutters. She explained how trauma falls into two categories: shock trauma (a single event like a car accident) and developmental trauma (a series of events compounded over time). She talked about the overextended fight-or-flight response that stutterers often have, and she shared a quote from the PTSD specialist Michele Rosenthal: "Trauma creates change you don't choose. Healing is about creating change you do choose."

Friends represents the very best of the stuttering community. Everyone is there to help. All week long, parents who had read my article would approach me between sessions and ask for advice in dealing with their son or daughter. Nearly all of these moms and dads had the same look in their eyes, a mix of compassion and fear. Over and over, parents presented versions of the same fundamental questions: *What is my son thinking? What does my daughter actually want me to say?*

I didn't really know what to tell them, other than to treat their kids like adults. I reminded them that young stutterers are forced to navigate so much on a daily basis, and therefore they grow up very fast. I listened as parents recounted in vivid detail how their child struggles to participate in class, how they fight to answer the phone. And I get it. I can't imagine how hard it is to watch your kid struggle to talk and know people will belittle them. But what I tried to tell these parents is that what they're witnessing at a restaurant is one of fifty such interactions in a given day, that they're not around to protect their child during the other forty-nine. This is a hard truth to hear, but it's not meant to be upsetting. I want parents to understand that however strong they believe their son or daughter to be, the reality is, they're fifty times stronger.

ON THE FINAL DAY of the convention, a variety of props appeared under a big tent in the parking lot next to the hotel. Lee, the organizer, asked Grace and me to post up behind a mock deli counter. Grace put on an apron and I wore a big white chef's hat. We had little plastic slabs of meat and a hand-drawn menu. Kids would walk up to us and place an order. The goal of the exercise was to desensitize young stutterers to this scenario and encourage them to not hide from articulating what it was they really wanted. We tried to keep it fun and lighthearted, but occasionally a kid would block hard on a sound and walk away in frustration. Several parents watched from a few feet away with glassy eyes. I was fighting the urge to cry myself.

All week long I kept running into a stutterer about my age named Alexander Burday, who grew up in New York but now lives out west. Alexander is tall, tan, and tattooed, with huge muscles. Everything about him is physically intimidating, but after a minute of conversation, you realize he's a gentle giant. When the deli exercise was over, I took off my chef's hat and went back into the hotel. Alexander and I passed each other in the hallway.

"Hey, man," he said. He smiled softly. I told him about the kids I was just practicing with outside, and about their parents looking on. Alexander is like me and so many others in that his family never really knew how to handle his problem. One way he dealt with it was to become a speech therapist himself. Standing in the hallway, as Alexander and I looked at each other, something inside me started to collapse.

"I, uh, I just . . ."

There was a lump in my throat. I didn't know what I was trying to say. He didn't rush to help me find the words. He just kept looking at me and waiting. He took a deep breath, then another, then another. I tried to talk again and started to cry. I looked down at the floor and wiped my eyes on my shirtsleeve. Tears kept flowing. I looked back at him. His face hadn't changed. He was just standing with me, letting me let it out. I was sobbing now. Alexander asked if he could give me a hug and I cried into his right shoulder. He didn't say anything. He just kept breathing slowly and deeply until I let go.

An hour or so later we're all standing at the bridge. Now it's finally my turn to walk up to the mic. I raise it toward my face and awkwardly exhale. A squeak of feedback echoes through the PA system. I start to block on my first word and instinctively look down at my feet. When the word finally comes I force myself to look back up at the crowd.

I tell the dozens of stutterers around me, and the parents, and the therapists, that no matter how much your family loves you—and they do—they may never truly understand what it is you go through. I block, and look away, and strain to look back up.

"But at some point . . . that has to be okay."

FRIENDS MOVES AROUND every year—that summer the convention was in Colorado. I had flown out for the week to experience it, but also to spend time with a particular stutterer who lived in the area: Hunter Martinez.

The morning after the conference wrapped, I drove down to meet Hunter in Parker, about twenty-five miles southeast of Denver. He had an extremely firm grip when we shook hands at the door of one of his favorite taprooms. There were dark bags under his eyes, but Hunter was energetic and in high spirits. He ordered a huge burger and a frosty beer. We sat at the restaurant for more than two hours, talking about stuttering and the latest updates on his cancer journey. We eagerly shared our plans for the rest of summer. Hunter, his wife, Jessica, and daughter, Harper, were getting ready to fly to Asheville, North Carolina, the next day. They had spent the previous weekend with friends in Crested Butte, and, not long before that, Hunter and Jessica had celebrated their sixth wedding anniversary in Maui. He seemed light.

Hunter was approaching the one-year anniversary of his diagnosis. He had so far powered through more than twenty rounds of chemotherapy. The treatment had greatly reduced the size of his tumors, but they had nonetheless metastasized—the cancer was still present in his liver and lungs. Hunter told me he was frustrated to have reached what felt like a plateau. But he was waking up every day and living his life. And he was gregarious and speaking confidently in the face of his stutter.

After lunch Hunter invited me back to his house. Inside, Jessica was doing laundry and getting ready for their trip. Harper was just waking up from a nap. We sank into the living room couch and played with his dog. Hunter commented on how I became significantly more disfluent when I first started talking to Jessica, someone whom I'd just met, but that my (relative) fluency returned the more I spoke with her. I smiled. I asked Jessica if she ever noticed the same thing about her husband when meeting new people. She said yes and we all laughed.

In October I texted Hunter during a nail-biter ending to a Dallas Cowboys game, knowing he was a lifelong fan. "Praying for your blood pressure," I wrote. He laughed and said he was being a good dad and putting Harper down to sleep—that he hadn't even seen the stressful plays in question. We started catching up on life. "Treatment is going well," he said. "Making good progress."

We traded a handful of warm text messages three days before Christmas, then again right before New Year's. Things were a little different now. He was still "on the chemo train," as he called it, but was also preparing for another round of surgery. "They are going to insert a radiation device in my lumbar and cement to strengthen the back," he texted. "No set date yet but probably next week." I told him I would keep him in my thoughts, and that I wanted to do a long catch-up over the phone when he was feeling a little better. "Sounds like a great idea to me!" he replied.

Two weeks later I texted him. A few hours went by without a reply, something that had never happened before. When a new message finally popped up on my phone, I momentarily stopped breathing. The text was from Jessica, not Hunter.

I OFTEN THINK BACK to the very first email Hunter wrote me in November 2019. It arrived a few hours after my Biden story appeared online. "As an attorney it is sometimes very hard to be a stutterer and work in this profession. I worry that sometimes my clients and fellow attorneys fear that I do not have the necessary knowledge," he wrote. "Thank you so much for your profile. It means a lot to me and I am sure countless other stutterers."

When I drew up a list of people I hoped to interview for this book, I put a few words next to each name—"Colorado lawyer who stutters" was what I had initially typed next to Hunter's. After our first conversation, I added notes about his cancer journey, which had just started. But each time Hunter and I talked I came to understand a new dimension of him.

Hunter wasn't merely a lawyer, or a cancer patient; he was a loyal friend and a devoted family man. The last thing he posted on Instagram, two days before Christmas, was a video of Harper taking her first steps. She waddled around a table in pink overalls, clapping and smiling. Chief among the many things Hunter Martinez was: a beaming dad.

"A lot of people had no idea how sick he was, because that's just kind of who he was," Jessica later told me. "He didn't want people to worry about him. He just wanted people to think of him as Hunter."

It dawned on me that this was exactly how he had lived his life as a stutterer.

28

Brothers

My brother knew that I was writing this book, but we still couldn't bring ourselves to talk about it. At my nephew's birthday party, a few people asked how my project was coming. Matt was in earshot of the conversation, and when I began to speak, it seemed like he intentionally walked away. I can't really blame him.

For a while, our texts had been brief. We'd share an update on our lives in a stilted, formal fashion, usually about something innocuous. And then I would start and stop a different version of the same sentence. I could picture my three little dots flashing then vanishing on his phone.

I couldn't finish my manuscript without speaking with him. It had been two years since I publicly faced my stutter, three since our night at the sports bar. At one point during the pandemic I was talking to a new stutterer almost every night. These conversations would go on for an hour, or two, or three. I told these fellow stutterers things I had been afraid to say to almost anyone else—especially my family.

A few weeks after I got home from Colorado, I texted Matt, telling him that I was thinking of heading to D.C. for a visit. I didn't mention the prospect of a conversation about our past, or about my stutter. He was friendly.

Hey John! All clear next weekend, will be great to catch up.

A week later, I texted again, letting him know I was going to stop at our parents' house for a couple nights on my way down from New York. Now I was psyching myself up to finally say it. I started typing out a new text: *Maybe we can talk . . .*

Then I saw his three dots appear.

Unrelated, if you are interested in chatting related to your book I certainly want to support and it is a good time for me for that.

Liz had offered to come with me, but this felt like something I should do alone. I left our apartment that Thursday and pulled into my parents' driveway after dinner. My mom had all my favorites waiting: pasta salad, hot chicken off the grill, Miller Lite in the fridge. A pan of brownies was covered in aluminum foil, cooling on the dining room table. She had folded fresh towels and stacked them in a symmetrical pile on the edge of my bed.

The next night, as she and my dad and I were coming back from a car ride, apropos of nothing, she said, "You'll see how Matt is such a great father." I let out a small sigh. It felt like my parents were going out of their way to make me see my brother in a good light. When I came down for breakfast the next morning, she had already made me a bacon, egg, and cheese on an English muffin. There was a hot pot of coffee on the kitchen counter and a little bottle of orange juice next to my plate. When we hugged good-bye, I could feel the transfer of her nervous energy. She didn't want her sons to be distant. I got in the car and started driving down I-95 toward Washington.

Matt suggested I meet his family late that afternoon for miniature golf at Hains Point, a little island on the Potomac River. As I drove through Rock Creek Park, I turned off the air conditioning and put the windows down. A storm had just rolled through the city. That metallic summer rain smell rushed into the car, steam rising from asphalt. My arms felt sticky. I arrived first and nervously waited. The plan was to get some playtime in with my nephews that afternoon, then talk with Matt at his house later that night, after the kids went to bed. When I saw their car turn into the lot, I hesitated to walk toward them. *Are we really gonna do this?*

SEVERAL HOURS LATER, I unlatched his side gate and walked around the back of the house. Matt was practicing golf swings in his yard under a string of globe lights. My nephew came bounding through the rear screen door in his pajamas. We all took turns hitting a few balls out into the cool, wet grass, then Jennie took him up to bed. As the door closed behind her, I could sense she wasn't going to come back out. Now it was just Matt and me.

We kept the small talk going for way too long. I'd look down, then up at the lights, then out toward the kids' play set. I kept waiting for the moment to finally segue us toward the past. Shortly after eleven, Matt beat me to it. He said he was happy to talk about whatever I wanted. It was the last thing I expected to hear.

I placed my iPhone faceup on the table between us and opened a new voice memo. I asked him for his permission to hit record. He looked at it and said, "Sure." I sat back in my chair.

"I don't . . . have any questions written down," I told him.

"I'm not approaching . . . anything to do with this project like . . . winners and losers." I told him what the past two years had been like, how I had been trying, for the first time, to stop hiding. I told him about Jim, and Lyle, and JJJJJerome, and Roísín, and Hunter, and others I had met. I told him how it seemed like almost every stutterer I was talking to had some sort of unfinished business with their family. I rambled, saying I wanted him to know that he wasn't on the witness stand. He listened. He nodded. I was struck by the fact that he wasn't interrupting me.

I brought up the first night we tried to talk about my stutter—and our past—back in October 2018. So much had changed in both of our lives since then. I asked if he felt any different right now than he did that night.

"I was defensive then," he said flatly. "I had my guard up big time. I honestly don't feel that way right now. I guess I feel like there could have been a much more mutual sort of sharing of perspectives and histories, even though it's without question who the aggrieved party in all of our childhood is, but even then I don't think I was arguing that."

I nodded. I glanced at my phone to make sure it was recording. I had my little green notebook and a pen resting in my lap—playing the part of a journalist—but they felt like movie props. Writing a book gave me a reason to be here, a purpose, but I also felt a little foolish, as if I were wearing an old brown fedora with a little white PRESS card on the side. You shouldn't need a whole apparatus to sit down and talk with your brother.

At the time of our sports bar conversation, three years earlier, I had been going to therapy for several months. I hadn't yet met Liz. Back then, Matt was the father of a two-year-old.

But now he had a second son, born barely a month into the pandemic.

"I didn't just have a second kid—I had another son four years apart from my first," Matt said. He was gesturing at the symmetry of our own age difference. "You think he looks like me; I think he kind of looks like you," he said. "That parallel, and being home to really be overwhelmed by that parallel throughout this whole pandemic, has been really, really influential on me," he said. He looked out toward his yard. "I can never claw back so many of the moments I'm ashamed of and came up so terribly disappointingly short on as a kid, but in the way the world has a weird way of doing this stuff, I've been given this opportunity to see to it that two other boys, four years apart—brothers—have a better childhood together, have a better relationship as kids. I can't tell you what a priority that is to me."

I thought about earlier that afternoon, how I had approached his car, how we had shared an awkward hug. He seemed nervous to be around me. Almost scared. I could feel the back of his shirt was already damp with sweat. These types of outings used to bring out the worst in my brother—anything remotely competitive would set him off. He'd curse, he'd throw clubs, he'd have a meltdown in the car on the way home. But here we were, and he didn't even want to keep score. He was patient with everyone, cheering everyone on. His youngest son kept wobbling up the greens and stealing my ball and walking away with it. When we finished the round, Matt had beers and snacks waiting. He was calm. He was loving. He seemed like he wanted to take care of everybody.

I had glimpsed this version of my brother a few times before. When I was seventeen, near the end of my junior year of high school, Matt invited me to stay the night down at his college apartment. We drank Coors Light and smoked weed and played beer pong with his friends and, late at night, walked across the street for greasy cheesesteaks. I stuttered around his crew, but that was the first night it didn't seem to matter to him. He had recently turned twenty-one. That afternoon, before I went down, he had written me an earnest letter in which he promised never to torment me or my stutter ever again.

As we sat in his backyard, I brought up that memory. I asked what had changed, what made him suddenly want to have me around out of the blue. He shook his head.

"I'm embarrassed," he said. "I'm ashamed that it took that long and that there were so many missed opportunities along the way."

It is amazing what a simple expression of contrition can do. The relief that came from hearing those words was enough to open my mental aperture to allow more positive images of our past to come into focus. I remembered how he had trekked to Penn State for a few football weekends, how he had flown out to visit me when I lived in Denver.

He started talking to me about his teenage years. He told me about feeling that he was on the outside looking in on the intimidating "lax bro" crew at his own all-boys school. Around that time, my uncle gave our family an old Mitsubishi pickup truck to use as a second car. When one of my parents would pick up Matt at school in the truck, he'd duck down so no one would see him. He told me how he was ashamed of his bad skin and other issues, and how he had turned that anger on me.

"I felt less-than, and I wanted to have this résumé as sharp as it could be. And being seen in the Mitsubishi truck or, you know, shamefully, having a brother with, uh—" He paused. "Uh . . . *a challenge* . . . or having a house not in the same neighborhood as theirs, anything that I saw was a potential ding on my 'score,' I pushed down."

He paused.

"I have to be careful, because I'm not trying to say, 'I don't even know that person,'" Matt said, referring to his younger self. "I look back at him and I *feel* like I don't know that person," he said. "It *does* bother me that I was that person in those years, and I can't get them back. And that's part of what I said about my sons—that it's some sort of poetic opportunity to really look after that relationship, and how they treat people, and how they just navigate the same years of their lives."

I brought up a hard phone call between us. In November 2019, a few days before my Biden story came out, I contacted Matt to tell him that there was exactly one sentence in the article along the lines of "my brother used to make fun of me." That was an understatement; I didn't want to get into the depth of his bullying in that piece. In a way, I've always felt an instinct to protect my brother's feelings. I love him. He loves me. Still, he was upset to have the sentence in there at all. Later that week, when he finally read the full article, something began to click. Little by little, he started to understand the weight of my stutter in a way he previously hadn't.

It was hard for him to watch me on TV. He was proud, but still uncomfortable being a captive audience as I struggled to speak. And yet, I remembered how Matt had reached out to me after watching thirteen-year-old Brayden Harrington stutter during the 2020 Democratic National Convention. It was a moving moment; I can't imagine summoning that sort of courage at Brayden's age. Matt told me that watching Brayden had jolted him, and that he was proud of me for being a leader in this community. A lot of people texted me right after Brayden spoke, but that message from my brother meant the most.

As we sat across from each other in his backyard, I told Matt that I feel lucky and fortunate that I have Liz, and good friends, and that I'm able to work.

"You're not lucky and fortunate," he said. "That makes it sound like it just landed on you. You created this with a fortitude and bravery that I do not have. And I would not have made it through. I would not have managed this, persevered through this. I think 'overcome' is fair because it doesn't mean 'beat it,' it means—"

"You can overcome the *fear* of stuttering," I said.

"Yeah, and you've got a full life. Don't call it luck and fortune. It's just, it's incredible fortitude and bravery, is really what it is. I don't know that I'll ever be able to understand what you've been through, I find it overwhelming, to be honest."

Later in the night, I told Matt about the many stutterers who have shared their stories of depression with me. For the first time ever, I told him about the depression I came to know not long after our family's move. He got upset.

"I'm just sorry I wasn't there for you more during that time," he said. "I really am. I just, that's just—something about a child being in pain fills my eyes up as a parent now. And I'm sorry I wasn't there for you. Not to mention I made it worse. I'm just sorry. That's all I can say." He said it again a couple of minutes later. "It hits home," he said. "I'm just sorry."

Then I paused for a while, but it wasn't a block.

"If I'm going to . . . actually believe that I have come a long way . . . on my journey as a person who stutters, with acceptance, and confidence . . . and understanding myself—I have to open my mind and my heart . . . to believing other people are also capable of change," I said. I paused. "And people who have hurt me."

I was looking him square in the eye now.

"That's easier said than done. But it would be . . . hypocritical of me, it would be foolish of me, ignorant of me . . . to think that I'm capable of change . . . and another person . . . isn't, you know?"

"Yeah," Matt said.

"And so I . . . want you to know that."

My sentence hung in the air for a moment.

I said I could finally acknowledge that neither of us will ever be able to change our past. I told him I don't want to reach old age and still be consumed with resentment and anger, and that it's a lot easier to let go when you feel someone is truly apologizing, like he was doing in his backyard tonight. He told me he understood.

"At least from my end, I want you to know that, even when things were shitty—because of me—you know, I still would have done anything for you at any moment, and that's still true," he said. "I'd sell this house for you tomorrow. And I did a shitty job of showing that for most of our time living together. But I hope that you believe that, because it's true."

I told him I believed him.

It was just after one in the morning. "Whoa," Matt said, looking at the clock. He couldn't believe how much time had passed.

I closed my notebook and rested my pen on the table. Then I leaned forward and hit stop on the recorder. We sat outside for a while and kept talking, just as brothers this time.

Acknowledgments

Thank you to my editor, Jonathan Segal, who believed in this project long before I wrote a word of the proposal. Jon has helped me for many years, offering wisdom and advice during long lunches and long-distance phone calls. No matter the scenario, Jon responds to a problem with compassion. He gracefully guided me as I struggled with the most challenging material in this book and pushed me to never lose sight of my end goal.

I'm humbled and honored to publish this book with Jon and with Knopf. Thank you to Reagan Arthur, Jordan Pavlin, Gabrielle Brooks, Laura Keefe, Sarah Perrin, John Gall, Amy Ryan, Daniel Novack, and the entire Knopf team for the quality and care you bring to the bookmaking process—and for the profound support you show your authors. It feels surreal to have my name printed alongside Knopf's name. And a special thank you to Oliver Munday for designing such an eloquent book jacket.

Thank you to my agent, Amelia Atlas, for your support and insight every step of the way. One pre-pandemic day, Molly and I met for coffee, and I told her I had an idea for a book called *The Delay*. Without a moment's hesitation, she said, "*Life on Delay* is better." She was right.

This project was built around scores of sensitive interviews and conversations, the vast majority of which Matthew Engel transcribed for the better part of a year. Matt is a talented young journalist and I couldn't have reached the finish line without his assistance. I'm sincerely grateful to Annika Neklason for helping me synthesize complicated neurochemistry and the science of communication into (what I hope is) readable text about the medical aspect of stuttering. And I'm indebted to Hilary McClellen for her meticulous fact-checking work on items large and small.

The Atlantic is a dream home for writers and editors and I'm forever proud to be a member of the staff. Thank you to Jeffrey Goldberg and Adrienne LaFrance for bringing me aboard and for encouraging me to pursue my goals. I'm grateful to all my *Atlantic* colleagues, past and present, especially Nick Baumann, Nora Kelly, Yoni Appelbaum, Juliet Lapidos, Denise Wills, Janice Wolly, Anna Bross, Helen Tobin, Ellen Cushing, and Shan Wang. Thank you to Laurie Abraham, the editor of my 2019 piece about Joe Biden and stuttering, for pushing me to lean into the nuance and gray areas of that assignment. And thank you to Yvonne Rolzhausen, Will Davis, Luise Strauss, Arsh Raziuddin, and Mark Peckmezian for all you did to make that finished story as strong as it could be.

Writing that article changed my life, and I wouldn't have been in a position to write that story, nor this book, had I not received a world-class education. Thank you to my elementary and middle school teachers at Holy Trinity, especially Ms. Celano, for giving us daily free-writing exercises. Because of Ms. Celano, I still see writing as something to look forward to, not dread (most of the time). Thank you to my English teachers at St. Joe's Prep, especially Mr. Patragnoni, Mr. Whelan, and Ms. Christian (R.I.P.). Thank you to everyone who helped me during my four years at Penn State, especially Paul Kellermann and Elizabeth Jenkins.

I'm grateful to all my past editors, managers, and internship coordinators for your endless patience when I knew next to nothing, especially Sarah Mobley at WXPN, Tim Whitaker at *Philadelphia Weekly,* and Eric Miller and Matthew Fritch at *MAGNET.* Thank you to Greg Moore, Kevin Dale, Ray Rinaldi, Tucker Shaw,

Suzanne Brown, Dana Coffield, Dan Petty, Anya Semenoff, John Ealy, Jason Blevins, Lisa Kennedy, Joanne Ostrow, Ricardo Baca, John Wenzel, John Moore, and Aaron Ontiveroz for helping make *The Denver Post* my first true home as a journalist. Thank you to Jim Brady and Robyn Tomlin for bringing me to New York to work for Digital First Media (and for all you did to help your employees find jobs when the layoffs came). Thank you to David Granger, Mark Warren, Jay Fielden, Michael Hainey, Michael Sebastian, Michael Mraz, John Sellers, Steve Kandell, Mike Nizza, John Kenney, Tom Junod, Charlie Pierce, and Eliot Kaplan for teaching me the craft of magazine journalism during my four years at *Esquire*. And thank you to Jason Fine, Sean Woods, Jerry Portwood, and Phoebe Neidl for warmly welcoming me into *Rolling Stone* and helping me fulfill a lifelong dream.

I consider myself extremely lucky to have found mentors who are not only exceptional journalists, but exceptional human beings. Thank you to Mike Sager for your years of writing advice, life advice, work-in-progress edits, and late-night phone calls of reassurance. Thank you to Josh Schollmeyer for taking a chance on me as an unknown freelancer and to Max Potter for vouching for me when we barely knew each other. Thank you to Jennifer Senior for intrinsically understanding the dynamics of this book from our first conversation (and for giving me a phrase that made it into the text). Thank you to Robert Kolker for lending your attentive ear during my eleventh-hour panic. Thank you to Patrick Radden Keefe for giving me the mantra that writing a book is really just waking up and putting one foot in front of the other until you reach the end. Thank you to Bill St. John—and several previously mentioned folks—for your early reads and invaluable feedback on this manuscript when it was just a bunch of white pages from my printer. And a special thank you to Dave Holmes who, when I was stuck in a rut, told me to write as if I were telling the story to just one person.

Thank you to all the stutterers, family members of stutterers, therapists, researchers, and people from my past who answered my request to let me interview you for this book. I feel so lucky to have been welcomed into the global stuttering community by the likes of Barry Yeoman, Joe Donaher, Tommie Robinson, Kia Johnson, John Moore, Eric Jackson, Chaya Goldstein, Mark O'Malia, Dhruv Gupta, Ryan Connors, Chris Schulyer, Aysha Ames, Matt Bernucca, Geoffrey Gertz, Emma Alpern, Will Blodgett, Caryn Herring, Kristel Kubart, Reuben Schuff, Kunal Mahajan, Chris Constantino, Michael Sugarman, Hope Gerlach, Derek Daniels, Jordan Scott, Jeff Shames, Lucy Reed, and Michael Sheehan. Thank you to all the members of the Brooklyn and Manhattan chapters of the National Stuttering Association for being there for me and each other, month after month. Thank you to Lee Caggiano and everyone at Friends, Heather Grossman and everyone at the American Institute for Stuttering, Tammy Flores and everyone at the National Stuttering Association, and Noah Cornman, Travis Robertson, Nathan Patterson, and the whole team at SAY.

Thank you to every single stutterer whose name appears in this book, especially Jim McKay, Gerald Maguire, Lyle Brewer, JJJJJerome Ellis, Roísín McManus, and Hunter Martinez (R.I.P.), for letting me interview you multiple times for multiple hours, and for trusting me to tell your story. Thank you to Courtney Byrd and the Kleon family for exemplifying a new way forward for young stutterers.

I spent a large chunk of the pandemic having nightly conversations with fellow stutterers from all over the world, and I wish I could have included all of their stories in the text. Thank you to Hannah Montañez, Will Nading, John Frank, José Ralat, Andrew Rogier, Jonathan Goldstein, Jeff Rose, Romtin Parvaresh, Kristina Harris, Devin Keezel, Felipe Frías, Meryl McQueen, Malik Abdalla, Christopher Questel, Kelvin Brooks, Sunilkumar Bombale, Heather McLeod, the Graf family, the Axelarris family, the Stone family,

Adam Steiner, Kelly Miller, Jack Tamisiea, Jared Richman, Tom Buday, Wisberty Velez, Stephen Gourley, Larry Stein, Rong Gong, Karin Granstrom, Bernard Glennon, Candace Adair, Thomas Williams, Audrey Hernandez, Christopher Coleridge, Alex Rosen, Erik Esinhart, Alyssa Mesich, Bill Graham, Ari Waldman, Attilio Spano, Edison Chilusia, Geoff Schwartz, Gabe Altman, Randy Panzarino, and Robert Grider for being so generous with your time and insights about our shared condition.

I'm indebted to every writer whose work has made an indelible impression on my life as a reader, especially David Carr, Tim O'Brien, Joan Didion, Mary Karr, and Richard Price. I would have never gotten this project done without a daily soundtrack of artists who reliably pull certain emotions out of me: Bob Dylan, Neil Young, Townes Van Zandt, Carole King, Thelonious Monk, Bill Evans, John Fahey, Wilco, David Berman, Jason Molina, the Replacements, and Thee Oh Sees, to name just a few. Though we've never met, thank you to Bing Liu for giving me the courage to interview my family after I saw you interview your mom in *Minding the Gap*. Similarly, thanks to Judd Apatow for all the life lessons you surfaced in *The Zen Diaries of Garry Shandling*, and to Ram Dass (R.I.P.) for reminding me that we're all just walking each other home.

Walking, itself, was a huge part of this book. My daily loops around Fort Greene Park were restorative, and I'm grateful to everyone who keeps the park in such excellent condition. Thank you to Not Ray's Pizza and Luigi's for your afternoon comfort slices. Thank you to Hungry Ghost for your procrastination coffee and La Bagel Delight for your restorative bacon, egg, and cheese on a roll. Thank you to Greenlight, Books Are Magic, McNally Jackson, The Strand, and every other New York bookstore for serving the city so well over the years. And thank you to Politics and Prose, Tattered Cover, BookPeople, Skylight, City Lights, Powell's, and all the other wonderful independent bookstores around the United States for creating such welcoming environments for anyone who loves to read.

I'm so grateful to my friends for being there for me long before I embraced my stutter—and for showing me endless support every day thereafter. My life in New York is made whole thanks to so many people, especially Kevin Rochford, Ryan Bort, Ben Collins, Matt Miller, Caprice Sassano, Ben Boskovich, Brendan Klinkenberg, Joe Murphy, and Meredith Martin. And I will always cherish those friends who have remained close despite geographic distance, especially Andrew deMichaelis, Dan Uminski, Emily Teele, Mike Lloyd, Colin St. John, and Ryan Johnson.

Thank you to Carole and Doug Rawson for being the best and warmest in-laws a person could ever ask for, and to Bobby, Danny, and Natalie Rawson for accepting me into your family from day one. Thank you to all my aunts, uncles, and cousins for looking out for me over the years. Thank you to my sister-in-law, Jennie, and my nephews, J and T, for bringing so much joy to the larger Hendrickson family.

I'm overwhelmed with love and gratitude for my mom, my dad, and my brother, Matt. It takes a remarkable level of courage and selflessness to allow a family member to write about the family. All three of you not only supported my endeavor, but willingly participated in this project. I don't know if I'll ever be able to repay you for that, but know that I'm thankful every day for your profound love and support.

And lastly, thank you to Liz Rawson, who began this project as my girlfriend and ended it as my wife. I'll never have the adequate words to describe how much you mean to me. You turn any challenge big or small into something we can face together. You are more than my life partner; you're my soulmate. I'm thankful you exist. I'm so glad I found you. I love you.

Notes

Chapter 1: Nothing in Your Hands

Author interview with Jeffrey Goldberg.

Chapter 2: Dead Air

Author interviews with family, Trish Bickford Petty, Dr. Scott Yaruss, Christine Samson Southern, and Dhruv Gupta.

9 Only since around the turn of the millennium: Lydia Denworth, "The Stuttering Mind," *Scientific American,* August 2021.

9 core stuttering "problem": Kate E. Watkins, Stephen M. Smith, Steve Davis, and Peter Howell, "Structural and functional abnormalities of the motor system in developmental stuttering," *Brain,* January 2008.

9 We start developing our ability to speak: Mayo Clinic Staff, "Language development: Speech milestones for babies," Mayo Clinic, https://www.mayoclinic.org/healthy-lifestyle/infant-and-toddler-health/in-depth/language-development/art-20045163.

9 Our little coos and babbles: Suneeti Nathani, David J. Ertmer, and Rachel E. Stark, "Assessing vocal development in infants and toddlers," *Clinical Linguistics & Phonetics,* July 2006.

9 Between 5 and 10 percent: National Institute on Deafness and Other Communication Disorders, National Institutes of Health, https://www.nidcd.nih.gov/health/stuttering.

9 between the ages of two and five: "What is stuttering?," WebMD, https://www.webmd.com/parenting/stuttering#1.

9 For at least 75 percent: "Stuttering," National Institute on Deaf-

ness and Other Communication Disorders, National Institutes of Health, https://www.nidcd.nih.gov/health/stuttering.

9 If you still stutter at age ten: Gavin Andrews, Ashley Craig, Anne-Marie Feyer, et al., "Stuttering: A review of research findings and theories circa 1982," *Journal of Speech and Hearing Disorders,* August 1983, 228.

9 an umbrella term: Denworth, "The Stuttering Mind."

10 move enough air through your lungs and larynx: Kristofer E. Bouchard, Nima Mesgarani, Keith Johnson, and Edward F. Chang, "Functional organization of human sensorimotor cortex for speech articulation," *Nature,* February 20, 2013.

10 three million Americans talk this way: "FAQ," The Stuttering Foundation, https://www.stutteringhelp.org/faq.

10 It's partly a hereditary phenomenon: Lisa Scott, "A look at genetic and neurological correlates of stuttering," *The Stuttering Foundation Newsletter,* January 2006.

10 A little over a decade ago: Denworth, "The Stuttering Mind."

10 clear dominant or recessive pattern: Carlos Frigerio-Domingues and Dennis Drayna, "Genetic contributions to stuttering: The current evidence," *Molecular Genetics and Genomic Medicine,* March 2017.

10 when it comes to identical twins: Denworth, "The Stuttering Mind."

10 The average speech-language pathologist: "Who Are Speech-Language Pathologists, and What Do They Do?," American Speech-Language-Hearing Association, https://www.asha.org/public/who-are-speech-language-pathologists/.

10 Of the roughly 150,000 SLPs: "Speech-Language Pathologists," *Occupational Outlook Handbook,* U.S. Bureau of Labor Statistics, https://www.bls.gov/ooh/healthcare/speech-language-pathologists.htm.

Chapter 3: The Look

Author interviews with family, Liz Rawson, Dr. Tommie Robinson, Dr. Kia Johnson, Andrew deMichaelis, and Christine Samson Southern.

18 percent of people: "Facts About Stuttering," National Stuttering Association, https://westutter.org/facts-about-stuttering/.

19 playing a part on an invisible stage: Erving Goffman, *The Presentation of Self in Everyday Life* (New York: Anchor Books, 1959), xi.

19 people wince as the stuttering public defender: *My Cousin Vinny,* directed by Jonathan Lynn (Twentieth Century Fox, 1992).

20 "The JJJJ-JJJaps are here!": *Pearl Harbor,* directed by Michael Bay (Touchstone Pictures, Jerry Bruckheimer Films, 2001).

21 No two stutterers: "Stuttering 101," SAY: The Stuttering Association for the Young, https://www.say.org/stuttering-101/.

21 an awkward exchange: Goffman, *The Presentation of Self in Everyday Life,* 12.

22 "At such moments": Ibid.

24 Many health insurers don't cover: "Private Health Plans," American Speech-Language-Hearing Association, https://www.asha.org/public/coverage/php/.

26 infamous D.C. graffiti artist: Paul Hendrickson, "Mark of the Urban Phantom," *The Washington Post,* October 9, 1991.

27 "Don't make me run": "Lisa on Ice," season 6, episode 8, *The Simpsons,* directed by Bob Anderson (Gracie Films, Twentieth Century Fox Television, 1994).

27 "Aurora borealis?": "22 Short Films About Springfield," season 7, episode 21, *The Simpsons,* directed by Jim Reardon (Gracie Films, Twentieth Century Fox Television, 1996).

27 "Back to the hammocks": "You Only Move Twice," season 8, episode 2, *The Simpsons,* directed by Mike Anderson (Gracie Films, Twentieth Century Fox Television, 1996).

Chapter 4: Balls and Strikes

Author interviews with family, Andrew deMichaelis, Emily Blunt, Alex Brightman, and Julie Brandenburg McGaffin.

29 "The streak almost ended": Richard Justice, "It's Over: Ripken Sits Out After 2,632 Games," *The Washington Post,* September 21, 1998.

32 syllable-timed speech: Natasha Trajkovski, Cheryl Andrews, Mark Onslow, et al., "Using syllable-timed speech to treat preschool children who stutter: A multiple baseline experiment," *Journal of Fluency Disorders,* March 2009.

33 we use different neural pathways: Per Alm, "Stuttering and the Basal Ganglia," The Stuttering Foundation, Winter 2006, https://www.stutteringhelp.org/stuttering-and-basal-ganglia.

Chapter 5: The Fluency Factory

Author interviews with Anne Oberhelman, Bill Oberhelman, Dr. Ron Webster, Chris Cochran, and Dr. Scott Yaruss.

40 The before-and-after videos: "HCRI Client Videos," Hollins Communications Research Institute, https://www.stuttering.org/alumni-videos-stuttering-therapy-at-HCRI.php.

41 people don't stutter when they sing: "Singing and Stuttering: What We Know," The Stuttering Foundation, https://www.stutteringhelp.org/content/singing-and-stuttering-what-we-know-0.

41 Elvis Presley, Bill Withers: "Famous People Who Stutter," The Stuttering Foundation, https://www.stutteringhelp.org/famouspeople.

41 Ed Sheeran would rap: Ed Sheeran's speech at the 2015 American Institute for Stuttering Gala, https://www.youtube.com/watch?v=K_3r3SolyDs.

41 Kendrick Lamar was a stutterer: Lizzy Goodman, "Kendrick Lamar, Hip-Hop's Newest Old-School Star," The New York Times Magazine, June 29, 2014.

42 "Country rooaaaddsssss": Bill Danoff, Taffy Nivert, and John Denver, "Take Me Home, Country Roads," John Denver, Poems, Prayers & Promises (RCA, 1971).

42 This also applies to recitation: Michael Kiefte and Joy Armson, "Dissecting choral speech: Properties of the accompanist critical to stuttering reduction," Journal of Communication Disorders, January–February 2008.

42 tens of milliseconds: Kristofer Bouchard, Nima Mesgarani, Keith Johnson, and Edward Chang, "Functional organization of human sensorimotor cortex for speech articulation," Nature, February 20, 2013.

43 That was the headline: "Virginia Psychologist Treats Stutterers by Computer-Assisted Therapy, but Some Experts Voice Doubt," The New York Times, March 27, 1972.

43 may be tied to a middle-ear issue: Ibid.

43 93 percent of its clients: "Gain Skills for Lasting Fluency with HCRI," Hollins Communications Research Institute, https://www .stuttering.org/index.php.

43 treated more than 7,000 stutterers: "About HCRI," Hollins Communications Research Institute, https://www.stuttering.org /overview.php.

44 Hollins's twelve-day intensive program: "The Cost of Your Stuttering vs. the Cost of Stuttering Therapy at HCRI," Hollins Communications Research Institute, https://www.stuttering.org /stuttering-blog/cost-of-stuttering-therapy/.

46 newscaster John Stossel: John Stossel, "Broadcaster John Stossel Discusses HCRI Stuttering Therapy," originally aired on Fox News; clip now posted on Hollins Communications Research Institute YouTube channel, https://www.youtube.com/watch?v =1VslpFyhRhM.

Chapter 6: Hard to Explain

Author interviews with family, Andrew deMichaelis, Peggy Celano, and Tony Braithwaite.

Chapter 7: Joe

Author interviews with family and Joe Donaher.

Chapter 8: Liquid Courage

Author interviews with Jim McKay and Joe Donaher.

Chapter 9: Black Waves

Author interviews with family, Mukesh Adhikari, and Gerald Maguire.

73 He was a consultant for the most recently revised version: Julie Cohen, "A new name for stuttering in *DSM-5*," *Monitor on Psychology,* July/August 2014.

74 "Everything": Thom Yorke, "Everything in Its Right Place," *Kid A,* Radiohead (Parlophone, Capitol, 2000).

77 Neurotransmitters are molecules: "What are neurotransmitters?," Queensland Brain Institute, The University of Queensland, Aus-

tralia, https://qbi.uq.edu.au/brain/brain-physiology/what-are
-neurotransmitters.

77 We can get a dopamine release: Erica Julson, "10 Best Ways
to Increase Dopamine Levels Naturally," *Healthline,* May 10,
2018, https://www.healthline.com/nutrition/how-to-increase
-dopamine.

77 stutterers have an imbalance of the activity of dopamine: Amber
Dance, "The new neuroscience of stuttering," *Knowable Magazine,*
September 2, 2020, https://knowablemagazine.org/article
/mind/2020/new-neuroscience-stuttering.

77 *blocking* the release of dopamine: Ibid.

77 GABA is another neurotransmitter: Annie Stuart, "GABA
(Gamma-Aminobutyric Acid)," WebMD, September 5, 2019.

78 GABA kicks in: David DiSalvo, "What Alcohol Really Does to
Your Brain," *Forbes,* October 16, 2012, https://www.forbes.com
/sites/daviddisalvo/2012/10/16/what-alcohol-really-does-to
-your-brain/.

78 Maguire and other researchers: Dance, "The new neuroscience
of stuttering."

Chapter 10: Kairos

Author interviews with family and Tony Braithwaite.

80 *The Boston Globe* published: Spotlight Team, "Scores of priests
involved in sex abuse cases," *The Boston Globe,* January 31, 2002.

81 resigned because of allegations: Martha Woodall, "A Difficult Year
for 'The Prep': Scandal, Departures Rattle St. Joseph's Prep," *The
Philadelphia Inquirer,* August 2, 2006.

81 pleaded guilty to two counts: Dan Morse, "Former priest put
on probation for fondling two Georgetown Prep students," *The
Washington Post,* November 10, 2011.

81 moved among several East Coast parishes: "Fr. Garrett Orr—
Archdiocese of Washington," Horowitz Law, https://adamhorowitz
law.com/fr-garrett-orr-archdiocese-of-washington/.

Chapter 11: Penn State, Part 1

Author interviews with Paul Kellermann and Samantha D (last name
withheld for privacy).

99 a raw account of Carr's decades-long struggle: David Carr, *The Night of the Gun* (New York: Simon & Schuster, 2008).

Chapter 12: A Hand Full of Wheel
Author interviews with family.

Chapter 13: Penn State, Part 2
Author interview with Paul Kellermann.

Chapter 14: "Sir! What Language Do You Speak?"
Author interviews with Allison Berger Hartman, Justin Berger, and Lyle Brewer.

113 psychedelic version of "The Star-Spangled Banner": Zachary Crockett, "The Invention of the Wah-Wah Pedal," *Priceonomics,* November 5, 2015, https://priceonomics.com/the-invention-of-the-wah-wah-pedal/.

Chapter 15: One-Way West
Author interview with Kevin Rochford.

Chapter 16: Borrowed Time
Author interview with Kevin Rochford.

127 "the indignity of being observed": E. B. White, *Here Is New York* (New York: The Little Bookroom, 1999).

130 *VICE* eventually moved in: Matthew Conboy, "'Goodnight Brooklyn': How Vice Media Killed Death by Audio," *The Daily Beast,* December 3, 2016, https://www.thedailybeast.com/goodnight-brooklyn-how-vice-media-killed-death-by-audio.

Chapter 17: "I Kind of Leave My Body"
Author interview with JJJJJerome Ellis.

133 the same East Village church: "St. Mark's Church in-the-Bowery," Literary New York, https://www.literarymanhattan.org/place/st-marks-church-in-the-bowery/.

134 Audience members couldn't tell: Sean Cole, "Time Bandit," *This American Life,* episode 713, act 1 (WBEZ Chicago, August 7, 2020).

134 "When I was first invited": Speech by JJJJJerome Ellis, St. Mark's Church in-the-Bowery, January 1, 2020.

Chapter 18: Pink Slips

Author interviews with Sherrod Small and Emily M (last name withheld for privacy).

141 said *The New York Times:* Ravi Somaiya, "Lofty Newspaper Project Is Closed After Two Years," *The New York Times,* April 2, 2014.

141 "Mr. Paton hears all sorts of clocks ticking": David Carr, "Newspapers' Digital Apostle," *The New York Times,* November 13, 2011.

Chapter 19: The Locked Box

Author interviews with Andrew deMichaelis, Emily M, and Stina P (last name withheld for privacy).

154 "Whatever happened to Gary Cooper?":"Pilot," *The Sopranos,* directed by David Chase (Chase Films, HBO, 1999).

155 the cameras take you inside Folsom State Prison: *The Work,* directed by Jairus McLeary and Gethin Aldous (Blanket Fort Media, 2017).

Chapter 20: "Our Bodies Betray Us"

Author interview with Liz Rawson.

170 "You can never quarantine the past": Stephen Malkmus, "Gold Soundz," Pavement, *Crooked Rain, Crooked Rain* (Matador Records, 1994).

Chapter 21: The Biden Letters

Author interviews with Joe Biden, John Burns, Michael Sheehan, Jeffrey Goldberg, Liz Rawson, and Hunter Martinez.

175 Trevor Noah had already: Trevor Noah, "Biden Gets His Trump Nickname and Stumbles Through His First 2020 Rally," *The Daily Show* (Comedy Central, April 30, 2019), https://www.youtube.com/watch?v=G82UsIzbuRs.

175 not unlike one that Fox News: Steve Hilton, "'Sleepy Joe' Biden stumbles through second Democratic debate," Fox News (Fox Corporation, August 5, 2019), https://www.youtube.com/watch?v=JgFF2GvWFf8.

181 "Former vice president Joe Biden": Stephanie Ruhle, *MSNBC Live with Stephanie Ruhle* (MSNBC, November 22, 2019).

Chapter 22: "It Just Didn't Deter Me"

Author interviews with Nathan Heller, Katherine Preston, Barry Yeoman, Morgan Housel, David Rogier, Marc Vetri, Michael Kidd-Gilchrist, Brandon Shell, Jeff Zeleny, and Tony Braithwaite.

190 "I have stuttered nearly all my conscious life": Nathan Heller, "The Stutterer," *Slate,* February 21, 2011, https://slate.com /news-and-politics/2011/02/the-king-s-speech-raises-more -questions-about-stuttering-than-it-answers.html.

191 "we don't seat people with speech impediments": Barry Yeoman, "Wrestling with Words," *Psychology Today,* November 1, 1998.

192 "When I cruised the piers": Barry Yeoman, "Tongue-Tied," *Out,* October 1997.

Chapter 23: "A Softer Place to Land"

Author interviews with Roísín McManus, Betty Altenhein, and Stavros Ladeas.

Chapter 24: "There Is No *Yet*"

Author interviews with Dr. Courtney Byrd, Meghan Kleon, Austin Kleon, and Owen Kleon.

204 the stutterer Arthur Blank: "University of Texas to create center to study stuttering," Associated Press, October 19, 2020.

Chapter 25: Mom and Dad

Author interviews with family.

Chapter 26: If Not for You

Author interview with Liz Rawson.

Chapter 27: Friends

Author interviews with Hunter and Jessica Martinez.

Chapter 28: Brothers

Author interviews with family.